What on Earth?

What on Earth?

*Considering the Social Implications
of Jesus' Sermon on the Mount*

BARNEY WIGET

WIPF & STOCK · Eugene, Oregon

WHAT ON EARTH?
Considering the Social Implications of Jesus' Sermon on the Mount

Copyright © 2022 Barney Wiget. All rights reserved. Except for brief quotations in critical publications or reviews, no part of this book may be reproduced in any manner without prior written permission from the publisher. Write: Permissions, Wipf and Stock Publishers, 199 W. 8th Ave., Suite 3, Eugene, OR 97401.

Wipf & Stock
An Imprint of Wipf and Stock Publishers
199 W. 8th Ave., Suite 3
Eugene, OR 97401

www.wipfandstock.com

PAPERBACK ISBN: 978-1-6667-3673-1
HARDCOVER ISBN: 978-1-6667-9548-6
EBOOK ISBN: 978-1-6667-9549-3

APRIL 12, 2022 8:09 AM

All Scripture quotations, unless otherwise indicated, are taken from the Holy Bible, New International Version®, NIV®. Copyright ©1973, 1978, 1984, 2011 by Biblica, Inc.™ Used by permission of Zondervan. All rights reserved worldwide. www.zondervan.comThe "NIV" and "New International Version" are trademarks registered in the United States Patent and Trademark Office by Biblica, Inc.™

Scripture taken from the Amplified Bible (AMPCE), Copyright © 1954, 1958, 1962, 1964, 1965, 1987 by The Lockman Foundation. Used by permission.

J.B. Phillips New Testament (PHILLIPS) The New Testament in Modern English by J.B Phillips copyright © 1960, 1972 J. B. Phillips. Administered by The Archbishops' Council of the Church of England. Used by Permission.

"Scripture taken from The Message. Copyright © 1993, 1994, 1995, 1996, 2000, 2001, 2002. Used by permission of NavPress Publishing Group."

Scripture quotations are taken from the Holy Bible, New Living Translation, copyright © 1996, 2004, 2007 by Tyndale House Foundation. Used by permission of Tyndale House Publishers, Inc., Carol Stream, IL 60188. All rights reserved.

Tree of Life (TLV) Translation of the Bible. Copyright © 2015 by The Messianic Jewish Family Bible Society.

"On earth as it is in heaven"

Contents

Preface | xi

PART ONE | WHAT'S THE BIG IDEA?

   What on Earth Is This "Heavenly Kingdom" About? | 7
   A Kingdom Needs a Constitution | 10
   An Upside-Down Kingdom | 12
   An Inside-Out Kingdom | 15
   Changed Hearts Change the World | 19
   The Inconvenient Politics of Jesus | 25

PART TWO | UTTERLY UPSIDE-DOWN ATTITUDES

   Blessed Are the Broken | 37
   The Groan of the Godly | 42
   The Collective "Ouch!" | 44
   The "Ouchless" Church | 51
   See You in the Mourning | 54
   Meekness: The Ego at Rest | 58
   Secure Enough to Serve | 61
   Half-Blind Eye Surgeons | 64
   The Meek and Name-Calling | 69
   The Costly Love of the Meek | 71

Love Without Limits | 74
More or Less Like Jesus | 78
Meek Enough to Love Those Who Don't Love Us Back | 82
The Third Way | 87
The Meek Witness | 91
Ravenous for Righteousness | 97
Better Rules ≠ Better Lives | 100
Righteousness for the Common Good | 103
"Rhodium" Rule Righteousness | 106
How Righteous Rebels Pray | 110
How Hungry? How Thirsty? | 118
Have Mercy—Will Travel | 120
Justice, Mercy's Sibling | 122
Mercy As a Verb | 126
The Merciful and Their Money | 130
Mammon Worship | 134
Mammon's Predatory Preachers | 137
Money Worries Mute Mercy | 140
Mercy Starves Mammon | 142
The Uncluttered Heart | 148
Healthy on the Inside | 150
Jesus on How To Treat Women | 152
Pure-Hearted Practitioners | 156
Single-Minded Seers | 158

Blessed Are Those Who Make *Shalom* | 162

Peace Be with You | 164

No Justice! No Peace! | 168

Shalom to Go | 170

The *Shalom*-Maker's Audacity | 173

The Empire Strikes Back | 176

Persecution: When It Is and When It Isn't | 181

Why Are They So Mad At Us? | 185

So, What Do We Do About It? | 189

PART THREE | WHAT ON EARTH?

Walk the Narrow Road | 195

Stay Clear of Broad-Way Preachers | 198

The Storm Will Tell | 201

Acknowledgements | 205

Bibliography | 207

Preface

The worst thing a book can do for a Christian is to leave him with the impression that he has received from it anything really good; the best it can do is to point the way to the Good he is seeking. The work of a good book is to incite the reader to moral action, to turn his eyes toward God and urge him forward. Beyond that it cannot go.

—A. W. Tozer[1]

I HOPE THAT THIS book is one of those books, a signpost for you and for me. I'm motivated as much by my own self-therapy as for *your* edification. I write as a fellow traveler. I still do wrestle with conceit as much as anyone, so if I exude an illusion of spiritual expertise it is not my intent. If I am ahead of you in the journey I invite you to join me. If you're ahead of me I urge you forward. Keep going and bring us with you.

This book is not meant to be a mere explanation of Jesus' words but an *invitation* into doing life with him. I don't want to just tell you what the Sermon on the Mount means. I want to join the Spirit as he beckons you into a meaningful life with those of us who are trying to follow Jesus.

"There are a lot of miracles in the Bible," says David Brooks, "but the most astounding one is the existence of that short sermon."[2] I've studied and taught through these three chapters in Matthew at least a dozen times during my life. I memorized it in college and have longed to understand it and live it ever since. Though my moral muscle memory is set to ways contrary to kingdom values, the Spirit perseveres in his efforts to reset those

---

1. Tozer, *God's Pursuit of Man*, 5.
2. Brooks, *Second Mountain*, 245.

reflexes of mine to inchmeal in order to reflect the ways of Jesus charted in these chapters.

With so much of it that I still don't grasp or practice to perfection, writing a book on it frightens me a bit. Since fear is no excuse for paralysis, I'll try to share what I currently see and leave you to the Spirit's guidance for the rest.

I will warn you that this Sermon, which is a condensation of some of the primary ethical teachings of Jesus, maybe more than in all his other discourses preserved for us in the New Testament, challenges our presuppositions about living the Christian life and calls us into an outlandish disciple's lifestyle. Taken intravenously, these three chapters in the book of Matthew will positively upset your equilibrium, invite you to muse, and challenge you to act.

"Why question me?" Jesus said to the high priest. "Ask those who heard me. Surely they know what I said" (John 18:21). Is it true that they knew? Surely *we* know what he said. Right? To our shame, a lot of us don't. There are an awful lot of biblically illiterate churchgoers these days. But the more relevant question is, will we *do* what he said? Furthermore, will we try to do *all* that he said or simply cherry-pick those items that suit us? That happens a lot with this particular discourse of Jesus.

It's been said and begs to be said again that it's time for a Christianity that looks more like Jesus! Neither his Sermon nor this book will automatically get you there. I know this because throughout all my years of reading and studying the Bible, along with reading hundreds of other books hasn't mysteriously transformed me from sinner into sainthood. But biblical knowledge plus collaboration between the Spirit and our will can produce better Christians.

We were originally hardwired to live the way Jesus prescribes here. Granted, with the break in our internal wiring, conduction is limited and our light shines intermittently at best.

Therefore, many readers blunt the sharp edge of this Teaching by romanticizing it as so much virtuous poetry. Many people have told me how much they love the Sermon on the Mount along with its fetching prose and lovely poetry. I have to wonder if they've actually read it! If they had, and I mean read it pensively with personal application in mind, I can't see how they could laud it as so much handsomely worded oratory.

Jesus didn't offer a sweet, syrupy spirituality for people who are looking for *a little more religion* in their lives. The Jesus that some people

Preface

seem to "love" is the one who makes no real demands on them and allows them to live any way they choose. *Just be nice to everyone, go to church once in a while, take out the garbage when it's full, and you're good to go.*

For some, the Discourse contains perhaps some of Jesus' most familiar teaching yet least followed. I suppose this could be explained by both nature and nurture. We inherited a contrarian nature from Adam and absorbed a defiant posture from all his children since. That must be why Jesus requires our death in order to walk in his way. If we want his way we have to "deny" our own and carry a cross around for ready access.[3]

Read it, soak in his words, observe the radical lifestyle he prescribes, die to your idols, and hold on to him for dear life!

---

3. Mark 8:34.

Part One

What's the Big Idea?

Christ, who preached this message twenty centuries ago, knew that he was sowing a long-term moral revolution in which we human beings come to change ourselves from worldly thinking.

—Oscar Romero

I've been trying to be like Jesus for nearly fifty years now. He's been kneading the shapeless dough of my heart into something that still only remotely resembles his. I'm coming along, albeit in a halting sort of way. I love him more than anything in the world but the way I think, speak, and act is still lightyears away from where I want to be.

I have two mantras that frame my efforts to live christianly. The first is this: *"The Christian life isn't hard to live. It's impossible! Only Jesus can do it!"*

Our jumble of human and divine natures has a lot to do with the impossibility of emulating him perfectly, not to mention the Grand Canyon-sized gap between our American way of life and his. Christianity, in contrast to the way of the world, seems like a totally upside-down approach to life.

Authentic faith is countercultural and therefore revolutionary. If you're shopping for one, you can find a shallow version of the faith that is substantially inferior to the Jesus version. Readily available is a Christianity whose "hands are the hands of Esau, but whose voice is the voice of Jacob."[1] This sort of flimsy faith is more palatable and therefore more accessible to

1. Gen 27:22.

people that prefer to be "spiritual" on their own terms. The Jesus version is not that.

The good news is that he doesn't expect us to rely on a superhuman ability of our own. His way is nothing if not *supernatural*, a life reliant on divine power from the inside out, which leads me to my second mantra: *"The Christian life is the life Jesus lived then, lived now by him in us."*

The likeness of Jesus is not something you tack onto your exterior. It's an *inside job*. His way of transforming us into his likeness is from *the inside out*. The white-knuckle approach to Christianity only leads to frustration and failure. We can only hope to live out the teachings of the Sermon on the Mount in the power of the *Savior on the Mount!*

The zeitgeist of today's evangelicalism is more dissimilar to the church we read about in the New Testament than I'd like to admit. Sometimes it bears little resemblance at all. With supposed Jesus followers drifting further and further away from our roots in biblical ethics, we need to take another serious look at his teaching on the hill that day, which radiates a blaze of light in every word.

E. Stanley Jones calls the Sermon "A working philosophy of life,"[2] wherein Jesus presents a new social possibility for the church and the world. The "Big Idea" of this book is this *new social possibility* found in these three chapters of Matthew's Gospel.

Most of the teaching I've heard (and personally given) focuses exclusively on the personal piety applications of these chapters. *Don't lie or lust or leave your wife. Forgive your boss for bullying and treat your coworkers with kindness.* While those applications are still as necessary as ever, if not much more, I intend to focus *this particular writing* on the ways Jesus challenges how we interact with contemporary culture morally, socially, economically, and yes, even politically. Viewed rightly, his revolutionary address proposes a counterculture kingdom that subverts conventional wisdom regarding how this world works.

"Martin Luther applied all the Beatitudes to the public sphere. For him, the Beatitudes concerned not only the Christian's life before God but the Christian's life before their neighbor."[3] The typical gospel of the contemporary evangelical narrative is predominantly individualistic. It's about how your sins are forgiven and how you become more *spiritual*. As biblical and magnificent as this is, apart from a vision to make the world a better place,

---

2. Jones, *Unshakable Kingdom*, 24.
3. Eklund, *Beatitudes through the Ages*, 374.

that good, yet *partial gospel* truncates the vision of God for the advance of his kingdom on earth. His vision is to make better people who in turn, with his supernatural potency, make a better world.

The metamorphosis of caterpillar to butterfly mirrors the radical change that Christ makes in those who receive him. The caterpillar is a consumer. Its day consists of eating its own leafy environment. When it "converts" into its ultimate form, it abandons its leaf and flutters from flower to flower, pollinating. Jesus didn't rise from the dead in order to create consumers but *pollinators* that effect change and bring beauty into the world. Besides, whoever hung a painting or photo on their wall of a chubby green caterpillar chowing down on a shrub, in place of an actual exquisitely decorated butterfly?[4]

At one point, Martin Luther King Jr.'s colleagues in the civil rights movement challenged him to stop speaking out on the Vietnam war. They wanted him to stick exclusively to the civil rights message. He rejected their advice and told them he refused to "segregate [his] moral concerns" between one mandate and another. It's all part of the same gospel of the kingdom and we should be able to hold these things in tension. For example, Pandita Ramabai fought for women's rights in India and at the same time, translated the entire Bible into her native tongue so those women could have a spiritual connection to God.

Similarly, friends of mine have advised me to stick strictly to the personal moral applications of Scripture—evangelism, disciple-making, prayer, and purity. I actually write and teach quite a bit about those things too. But, like King, I can't segregate my moral concerns between personal and social issues. I'm concerned about *all things biblical*, which unquestionably includes how I relate to God, to my family, to my church, and to my larger sphere of influence as a witness for Christ. But the gospel also clearly speaks to such issues as racial, economic, and political justice. In this book we'll focus on those sorts of things often overlooked in the reading of Jesus' most famous Sermon.

> Some streams of Christianity emphasize personal morality: don't sleep around, get wasted, or steal from your boss, and you should be all right. Other streams emphasize social justice: feed the hungry, stop racism, and end poverty. Unfortunately, we often tend to separate these streams and overlook one or the other. Jesus

---

4. My friend Chris Matley suggested this metaphor. Thanks, Chris!

confronts us by taking both streams and bringing them back together into a larger, rushing, raging river.[5]

I personally pledge allegiance to no political party, but hold ideals that would be considered Republican-ish and other ideals that make me look more like a Democrat. I don't check all the boxes underneath any party name at the top of a ballot. My goal is to be an independent, critical-thinking citizen of two kingdoms—the earthly and the heavenly.

I'm pretty sure that Jesus wouldn't have identified himself by a party platform either. Loving God and neighbor is what he was all about and must be the lens through which we make our moral, social, and political choices. I believe his politics are set forth in all his sermons, which neither the Right nor the Left rush to adopt. If he were given a vote, I'm pretty sure he would check only the boxes for candidates and proposals whose outcome would best lead to the glory of God and the good of people.

His is a revolutionary spiritual and social agenda, which clearly functions not on the basis of power but on divine love. He transforms the world not by force but by fascination, a playbook we would all do well to emulate.

In *To Kill a Mockingbird* Maudie said to Scout, "There are just some kinds of men who're so busy worrying about the next world they've never learned to live in this one, and you can look down the street and see the results."[6] The typical evangelical pitch to pre-Christians these days sounds something like, "Come to Jesus and when you die he will take you to a better world." While that's true, I believe that our presentation should include something more like, "Come to Jesus and you'll come alive. And when you do, come help us make this a better world!"

Of course, someday we'll go to the best of all worlds. Nevertheless, today our task is to make this the best world we can. Still, many Christians seem to think that aside from getting people saved and warning them of certain pet sins, our job is to sing songs, be polite, and hug one another until Jesus returns.

There aren't two gospels, a *salvation* one and a *social justice* one. Donald Kraybill said that "Jesus binds the spiritual and social into a seamless fabric that shouldn't be torn in two."[7] We can't rightly separate personal piety from working toward a society that's steeped in justice. Any split between *spiritual* and *social* leads to a warped view of Scripture and lacks a complete

---

5. Butler, *Skeletons in God's Closet*, 28.
6. Lee, *To Kill a Mockingbird*, 45.
7. Kraybill, *Upside-Down Kingdom*, 27.

compliment of kingdom ethics. We cut the salvation of Jesus in half when we ignore broken social systems and then try to serve that partial salvation to famished pre-Christians who recognize half a meal when they see it.

To many Christians, working for justice in this world is as futile as polishing the brass on a sinking ship. *If it's all going to sink anyway, why bother beating our heads against the wall to improve the living conditions here?* We bother, because this is God's comprehensive mission into which he invites us to collaborate with him.

What good is Christianity if all we do is complain about how bad the world is, pass the peace to one another during church, and preach about how to be prosperous while waiting for Jesus to come and take us out of this sinful place?

The Bible is replete with commands for believers to live *justly* in society and to preach this as an indispensable component of Christ's kingdom. Of all the sins that roiled the prophets, besides idolatry, *injustice* was at the top of their list. Scan the writings of Isaiah through Malachi and see for yourself.

Just take the so-called *Golden Rule*—wouldn't you think that treating others like we wish to be treated should affect our views and activities in reference to such issues as immigration policy, racial inequality, the taxation system, foreign policy, and even civility in public debate?

Richard Stearns suggests that our contemporary version of the gospel has a *hole* in it. "Being a follower of Jesus Christ requires much more than just having a personal and transforming relationship with God. It also entails a public and transforming relationship with the world."[8] It's a *full gospel* that does the world the most good.

You'll find our tour through the Sermon on the Mount to be more of a commentary on the church's influence on our culture than a line-by-line commentary on each verse of the text. While I sincerely hope to be true to Jesus' original intent and to base my conclusions on sound biblical exegesis, you won't necessarily find here the sort of verse-by-verse exposition of Matthew 5–7 that many brilliant scholars[9] have published over the years.

Our Big Idea is to address some of the more challenging social and civic implications of his teaching.

8. Stearns, *Hole in Our Gospel*, 5.
9. See bibliography

"Lord, help us make our lives an offering of quiet commitment to thread love through the torn garments of society. Amen."[10]

---

10. Claiborne, *Common Prayer*, 123.

What on Earth Is This "Heavenly Kingdom" About?

The Church exists to give the world a preview of coming attractions.
—Bryan Loritts

To thrive we must transcend our automatic responses and learn to see and act from a more complete and accurate understanding of reality. Jesus claimed that he understood the true nature of reality, which he called "the kingdom of God."
—Mark Scandrette[1]

We don't really get Jesus or his teaching without some clue about what he meant by his favorite term: "kingdom." Though this is no place to make a thorough topical exploration of the theme, I think a hasty primer might be in order.

Let's begin by confessing that we Americans know little to nothing about "kingdoms." It's pretty much limited to what we read in history books or what we watch on BBC Television. Given a lack of context, church folks typically use "kingdom" as a generic word to describe just about anything spiritual. But what are we actually talking about here?

---

1. Scandrette, *Ninefold Path*, 9.

Heaven Shares its King

In this Sermon Jesus uses "kingdom of heaven" over and over to describe a way of life that is transplanted from heaven to earth. It's not just a kingdom *in* heaven, but the kingdom *of* heaven wherein he injects the life of heaven into willing earthly subjects. He gradually grows that life inside us, and then through us plants it like seeds throughout the earth. His kingdom exists in heaven, and before heaven finally descends on earth in its totality, he kneads it into the earth through his subjects.[2]

In short, the kingdom is the "King's domain," the condition wherein King Jesus has "dominion." Any time you have people acknowledging his kingship and submitting to his authority you have the kingdom. The kingdom is not so much a *location* as a *condition*. When people embrace and advance the *kingship* of God, that's the kingdom of God.

When Jesus made his earthly appearance, he brought with him a whole new spiritual and social possibility, one in which all people are honored equally instead of sorted into classes, where enemies are loved, where resources are generously shared, and where power is put in the hands of the meek.

When Jesus sets up his headquarters inside us, relationships, households, economies, governments, and every feature of culture begin to lean toward heaven's standards. God's new social order infiltrating earth produces improved image bearers, healthier families, socially conscious business models, and governments that offer liberty and justice for all.

God's saving grace, which transfers us from one bad kingdom to the best of all kingdoms, remakes us in his image and reforms the world around us. Establishing a *shalom*-shaped community requires the same divine power as saving an individual from his or her sin and selfishness.

So What?

When Jesus said his kingdom is not *of* this world, he didn't mean it had no place *in* this world. In eternity he inhabited heaven's perfections and there ruled supreme. In history he came to earth to show us what perfection

---

2. As important as it is to know from whence this kingdom is launched, it's particularly pertinent to recognize where it lands and for which it is relevant. Jesus refers to "earth" six times in the Sermon (Matthew 5:5, 13, 18, 34; 6:10, 19).

looks like and to teach us how to emulate him while living here as citizens of both earth and heaven.

"What the world needs," says Shane Claiborne, "is people who believe so much in another world that they cannot help but enact it."[3] Our job is to provide the best possible preview of the future when Christ will return and reign as King over a new heaven and earth. After all, more times than not, Jesus calls his realm the "kingdom of heaven" and then teaches us to pray and live in such a way as for heaven to permeate the earth.

Just as a good movie's preview makes you want to go see the rest of it, we are tasked with imagining and demonstrating the reign of God in hopes that people will accept the invitation to come for the rest of the show and partner with us to make a better preview for all the world to see.

The skeptic of the Sermon says, "Our citizenship may be in heaven, but we have to live in this world now!" In other words, "This stuff won't work on earth. We'll have to wait till we get to heaven to get it right."

He's partially right, but as I often say, shoot for the moon and if you hit the trees, at least you got off the ground! Someday we will take our leave of this world and take up residence in the better one, but this Discourse is not about leaving earth and going to heaven. It's about bringing heaven to earth.

Jesus planted his flag in us, making us both *subjects* and *agents* of his heaven-like order. He works *in us as his subjects* in order to capture increasingly more territory in our hearts and he works *through us as his agents* to increase his kingly influence in the world.

Our King stresses progress in the way we live as individuals and in the way we organize our common life together. His is a vision of human flourishing and a society structured according to the will of God.

To him belongs the "Kingdom, the power, and the glory for ever and ever," yet he elected to bequeath to us "the keys"[4] that open the way for his kingship to proliferate on earth as it does in heaven. Though his kingship comes and his will is done not exclusively by human effort, it won't come without it. He assigns us the task of advancing his kingdom's reach and propels us with the power to do it.

---

3. Claiborne and Law, *Jesus for President*, 211.
4. Matt 16:19.

A Kingdom Needs a Constitution

The history of the impact of the Sermon on the Mount can largely be described in terms of an attempt to domesticate everything in it that is shocking, demanding, and uncompromising, and render it harmless.
—Pinchas Lapide, Jewish theologian

All social and governmental entities require a document that communicates the fundamental principles around which they choose to govern themselves. The revolutionaries of the New World knew they needed a way to articulate their vision for their embryonic society, some purposes and parameters for how they and their descendants were to live together. Every commonwealth needs a constitution in one form or another. Our Christian commonwealth is no exception.

Jesus explains more directly in this Sermon than in any other place in our New Testament the principles fundamental to our conduct before God and our potential contribution to the world. His *Constitution* is aimed way too high for humans living by purely human means. I'll say again that the Sermon on the Mount can only be lived in the power of the *Savior on the Mount*. While the drafters of our US Constitution could offer Americans no special power to practice the principles prescribed therein, the inwardly governed citizens of Jesus' commonwealth are empowered to lean into its prescriptions for liberty and justice for all.

We misunderstand his Teaching "if we look on it as the chart of the Christian's duty. Rather it is the charter of the Christian's liberty, his liberty to go beyond, to do the thing that love impels and not merely the thing that duty compels."[1]

Though culturally counterintuitive, the Jesus way is the way for which humans were originally constructed. We were made for this. It's our soul's *home*, the *air* we were meant to breathe. The One who made us knows what we're made of and made for. Hence, he has the inside track on how we must live and how to empower us to function for peak performance.

Though it may feel foreign at first, if we will give it a chance, we'll see it's the most natural way to live. "The eye was made for light, the ear for music, the heart for love, so our very being was made for Jesus' way of life."[2]

Why couldn't the teachings in the Sermon on the Mount be recognized as creedal? For theological orthodoxy we have the Apostles' and Nicene Creeds, yet you can recite them every week but remain unchanged. Can you imagine if the principles of Jesus' Teaching had been recited over the centuries, each time with conviction?

> *I believe in loving my enemies and blessing those who persecute me*
> *I believe in nonviolent resistance to injustice*
> *I believe in storing up my treasures in heaven instead of on earth*
> *I believe that before judging another it's best if I take the beam out of my own eye first*
> *I believe in a shalom-saturated society wherein we treat each other like we wish to be treated*

You get the point. One can only wonder how such a custom could transform the church and the world.

---

1. Jones, *The Unshakable Kingdom*, 56.
2. Jones, *The Unshakable Kingdom*, 122.

An Upside-Down Kingdom

These who have turned the world upside down have come here too. [They] are all acting contrary to the decrees of Caesar, saying there is another king—Jesus.

—ACTS 17:6–7

This Sermon challenges the whole underlying conception on which modern society is built.

—E. STANLEY JONES[1]

WE WHO MAKE OUR feeble attempts to emulate Jesus are viewed by the upside-down culture as the actual *upside downers*. It's a matter of perspective. God's ways, especially those prescribed in the Sermon on the Mount, are only "upside down" in proportion to a culture that thinks of itself as "right side up."

I heard that in the science of the human eye the image projected on our retina is upside down. I guess our brain compensates for it somehow and makes everything come out right. It doesn't really make a lot of sense to me, but since smarter people than me say it, I'll buy it. Maybe God's perspective in contrast to ours works that way.

Let me oversimplify it this way.

Back in a glorious Middle Eastern garden God created us "upright" until we unadvisedly took the word of his nemesis and defied the natural order of the Creator. We became inverted, and we've existed in this cockeyed

---

1. Jones, *Unshakable Kingdom*, 58.

An Upside-Down Kingdom

posture for so long now that we presume ourselves to be right-side up. We couldn't imagine another way to conduct ourselves until Jesus came along modeling an upright life and invited us to follow suit.

We call his way the "upside-down" way only because it appears in such contrast to the way we commonly conduct ourselves. It's so contrary to human nature and our faulty logic that it appears upside down to us. Appearances notwithstanding, from the very beginning his way was meant for our highest functionality. Any other way is unnatural and corrosive.

Jesus shattered stereotypes and upended norms. Peter Maurin, the eccentric cofounder of the Catholic Worker movement, said: "If I am crazy, it's because I refuse to be crazy in the same way that the world has gone crazy." Likewise, Paul the apostle unashamedly called himself a "fool for Christ."

In this kingdom the least are the greatest, adults become like children, and religious folk are apt to miss the heavenly banquet! Everything is reversed. Instead of vaunting themselves, true followers cut to the back of the line and invite others to take their place at the front. "Paradox, irony, and surprise permeate the teachings of Jesus. They flip our expectations upside down and completely upset our predictions."[2]

Rather than bowing tamely to cultural relevancy, Jesus instructs us to adopt the ethics of his inverted kingdom. Civil rights provocateur, Martin Luther King Jr., preached this in his message entitled, "Paul's Letter to American Christians":

> There are many Christians in America who give their ultimate allegiance to man-made systems and customs. They are afraid to be different. Their great concern is to be accepted socially. For so many of you morality is merely group consensus. In your modern sociological lingo, the mores are accepted as the right ways. You have unconsciously come to believe that right is discovered by taking a sort of Gallup poll of the majority opinion.[3]

As a result, much of our present-day American Christianity is tame and soppy. It doesn't resemble our controversial, troublemaking Leader, who challenged the status quo of his time. While Jesus offers us an alternative way of living in this world, we've largely domesticated what he dared to turn on its head. "The more we read the Gospels," says Kathy Escobar,

---

2. Kraybill, *Upside-Down Kingdom*, 23.
3. King, "Paul's Letter to American Christians," para. 9.

"allowing the Beatitudes to sink into our bones and be sewn into our skin, the more we realize that there's really nowhere else to go but down."[4]

Craig Greenfield has a poignant way of demonstrating Christ's way as an ethic where *up is down and down is up*:

> Where empire rides a white military horse and wields weapons of shock and awe, the upside-down Kingdom rides a donkey's back and says, "Love your enemy, even if he crucifies you."
>
> Where empire consolidates power and says, "My way or the highway," the upside-down Kingdom kneels with a towel and washes feet, saying, "I come to serve."
>
> Where empire honors the influential and celebrates the celebrity, the upside-down Kingdom welcomes little children and gives food to the hungry.
>
> Where empire is a rat race to the top, the upside-down Kingdom says the last should be first, losers are winners, and the most important among us will do the dishes.[5]

In this complete reversal of values, we who embrace his way discard what the world deems desirable and prize what it calls pitiable. Knowing that we were made for a better way, it should come as no surprise when we experience an increasing sensation that we no longer fit in with what is culturally commonplace.

> Don't become so well-adjusted to your culture that you fit into it without even thinking. Instead, fix your attention on God.... Unlike the culture around you, always dragging you down to its level of immaturity, God brings the best out of you, develops well-formed maturity in you. (Rom 12:1–2, The Message)

His way calls the standards of this world's system into serious question and leads us to a life of eternal abundance. Therefore, we choose to navigate against prevailing social winds and open our sails to the breeze of the Spirit.

---

4. Escobar, *Down We Go*, 28.
5. Greenfield, *Subversive Jesus*, 43.

An Inside-Out Kingdom

Be changed from the inside out. Readily recognize what he wants from you, and quickly respond to it.

—Rom 12:2, The Message

Be keener than ever to work out the salvation that God has given you with a proper sense of awe and responsibility. For it is God who is at work within you, giving you the will and the power to achieve his purpose.

—Phil 2:12–13, Phillips New Testament

I'M BOTH ENAMORED WITH and a bit frightened of Jesus' daring ethic. His message contains some of the most fetching words ever spoken and at the same time the most unachievable to live under the power of human steam. *Love your enemies, do something good for the person cursing you, and do it without telling anyone you did it.* Seems pretty out of reach to me!

His is a kingdom of surprises. If you want to be "blessed" be poor, be sad, be meek, be hungry, be persecuted! As he shatters socio-spiritual stereotypes he beckons us into trusting him for assistance.

Jesus lived so radically that most of his contemporaries thought he was just the newest spiritual crank in a long line of cranks. Undeterred, he determined that his *upside downness* would not end with him. He would perpetuate it in and through those brave enough to enlist. Given our predisposition toward conforming to cultural norms his proposal is scandalous. Therefore, the only way for us who are so bent on our own preferences to practice his way of holy nonconformity is from the *inside out*.

He aims so high that in order to rationalize their low-lying lives, some interpreters *lawyer down* his demands. But as Clarence Jordan says, "High aims and high ideals never handicap us. It certainly would not have helped us if Jesus had lowered the Kingdom standards to the point where they would be within easy reach of the weakest person. If anything, this would've made us still more powerless. We need not lower our goals, but receive the strength to obtain the goals which are set."[1]

The only way he could replicate his lifestyle is to move in and take over the whole *house*. However, instead of depending on his impetus from within, many people with a shallow version of faith prefer some version of religious "outwardism."

Avoiding "Outwardism"

Jesus seems pretty intent on transforming people into whole humans, yet the refrain of the religionist is, "If you can't *be* good, at least *look* good!" On the contrary, Jesus said, "You look really good on the outside but you're like a freshly painted crypt full of rotting flesh."[2]

Don't get me wrong; you won't find Jesus downplaying outward behavior as though it doesn't matter. How we actually conduct ourselves in the world absolutely matters. He downloads in us whole files of clear dos and don'ts to live by, yet he insists that *the outward is the outcome* of something much deeper inside us that craves to bring pleasure to God. All things being equal, what he installs *inside* will show up on the *outside*.

But since he gave his mountaintop speech as an alternative and an antidote to flimsy religion, to misread it as a formula for outwardism is a grave mistake. Since *Phariseeism is the same yesterday, today, and forever* we just can't seem to resist taking off-ramps that lead to formulas and morphing our faith into a performance. Therefore, any legalistic interpretation of his Address is a miscarriage of its intended use.

Take, for example, the moral obligation to be generous with the disadvantaged. Those with the severest religion hire trumpeters to announce their every contribution.[3] Their reward consists only of the accolades of others in place of bringing pleasure to God. While Jesus prescribes a God-pleasing inwardly governed liberality, spiritual playactors posture for praise.

1. Jordan, *Sermon on the Mount*, 78.
2. Matt 23:25–28.
3. Matt 6:2.

An Inside-Out Kingdom

The Heart of the Matter

Jesus says that it's the "poor *in spirit*" that possess the kingdom and the "pure *in heart*" that see God. The adulterer first lusts "in his heart" before he acts on it in the flesh. Loving our enemies, not simply acting nice to them around the water cooler, begins in the heart. That which we "treasure" finds its way into our hearts and it's the good sap in our roots that makes its way to the tips of our branches and "bears fruit." This is the essence of God's inside-out project.

Only this Sermon's Preacher and those within whom he resides can practice what he preaches. Upside downers live *inside-out* lives. Jesus sits in the control center of the heart, prompting behavior that puzzles an onlooking world.

Exterior-only religion downplays or altogether discounts the innermost part of us. The human *spirit* is left out of many "Christian conversations" about what it means to be human. "Jesus insisted that people could not live at the circumference unless they were alive at the center," says E. S. Jones. "The modern attempt is to have quantity of life at the circumference regardless of quality of life at the center. Jesus knew this would end in futility and cynicism and utter shallowness."[4]

God designed us and has designs on all our parts. Spirit, soul, and body are all in play.[5] Trying to live like Jesus by simply denying the body and disciplining the soul, thus leaving our spirit almost entirely out of the process, is a sweaty business. But Jesus made it possible for God's transforming power to inwardly invade us so that our innermost being influences our outermost parts.

On the eve of his arrest he told his apprentices, "The prince of this world is coming but he has nothing in me,"[6] that is, Satan had nothing inside him that he could exploit. His spirit was so full of the Holy Spirit, which left no room for anything to which the Adversary could appeal, nothing inside him to hook in order to reel him in.

I wish I could say that about myself. The fact is, I have any number of *hookable* places in my soul, uncrucified passions and desires[7] that the

---

4. Jones, *Unshakable Kingdom*, 112.
5. 1 Thess 5:23.
6. John 14:30.
7. Galatians 5:24

enemy often exploits at will. I'm grateful for God's forgiveness—and for incremental improvement!

Those who practice a faith that looks more like behavior modification or sin management fail to understand that we are *inwardly determined*. The power that makes us more like Jesus on the outside is the life of Jesus on the inside. Our interior is a widely vaster realm than our exterior, one we would do well to cultivate.

Changed Hearts Change the World

Changing the human heart and changing human society are not separate tasks, but are as interconnected as the two beams of the cross.

—Henri Nouwen

Social radicalism apart from faith "has been like a cut flower without nourishment, without any sanctions deeper than human courage and good intentions."

—Walter Brueggemann[1]

For the first three hundred years or so, the Sermon on the Mount was so fundamental to the Christian community's way of life that it was their most often-quoted portion of Scripture. But when, under Roman Emperor Constantine, Christianity was largely co-opted by the state, the Sermon's interest among adherents of the faith declined. "The revolutionary Sermon began to lose its central place in the Church's teaching because it threatened those in power and subverted the authority of the empire."[2]

Jesus overturned more than temple tables; he upended cultural norms, challenged authorities, undermined the establishment, and shook up most everything and everybody in his wake. Many embraced his counterintuitive kingdom ethic. Others, unwilling to relinquish their social privilege and political clout, engineered charges against him and lynched him as a

---

1. Brueggemann, *Prophetic Imagination*, 65.
2. Greenfield, *Subversive Jesus*, 99.

Part One | What's the Big Idea?

criminal and insurrectionist. He taught his followers that in spite of facing a similar fate, they were to love and pray for their persecutors.

When Jesus moves in, he dismantles our personal ethics and replaces them with his inverted ones. But he doesn't stop there. He saves our souls and through us seeks to improve society. He destabilizes the defective foundation on which modern society is built and substitutes it with sturdier material. He was and is the kind of Carpenter that repairs the soul and renovates society.

When we say that we aspire to be like him, are we just talking about being clean-talking, drug-free, conservative-voting polite citizens? Or must we have something more in mind? Joshua Ryan Butler says, "Jesus calls us to holiness and justice. Holiness involves dealing with the spark, the poisoned well, the root in our own hearts. Justice involves dealing with the wildfires, the raging rivers, the wicked trees in our world."[3]

The prophets of old preached a message similar to the one Jesus gave. All those "seers," from Elijah to John the Baptist, *saw* something and *said* something aimed to upset the status quo. As they rowed against the current, they alerted all those floating by on their merry way downstream of their destructive ways, a ministry for which they paid dearly.

Jesus promised a blessing to his persecuted followers because they are treated like "the prophets who were before [them]."[4] The implication is that his followers are, on some level, the progeny of the prophets. Martin Luther King Jr. thought so and said that the church is "the conscience of the state . . . the guide and the critic of the state, and never its tool."[5]

High price tag notwithstanding, speaking truth to (and about) power is something the church needs to recapture. In a self-satisfied secular culture, "prophets" aren't particularly popular. People tend to hush an active critical conscience. Nevertheless, I agree with King (and *the King*) that it's time for us to disrupt the dysfunctional. As we strive toward a more perfect union, lawmakers and the media who frame public issues need the church to hold them accountable to the sort of eternal values reflected in the Sermon on the Mount.

Some will have to deconstruct their theology more than others in order to exhibit a kingdom lifestyle. I find myself constantly adjusting my

---

3. Butler, *Skeletons*, 32.
4. Matt 5:11–12.
5. King, "Knock at Midnight," para. 15.

perspective as the Spirit patiently walks me through the story, each time with greater clarity.

As I've indicated, we can't afford to bifurcate the spiritual and the social implications of the gospel. Splitting the two leads to a warped reading of Scripture and tempts us to domesticate the gospel. Any gospel without feet isn't the gospel at all. "Prayer and evangelism without social action," writes Father John Bettuolucci, "leads to pietistic withdrawal from the realities of the human condition and an escape from social problems rather than a confrontation and challenge to change."[6] "An individual gospel without a social gospel," said the great twentieth-century missionary to India E. Stanley Jones, "is a soul without a body, and the social gospel without an individual gospel is a body without a soul. One is a ghost and the other a corpse."[7]

One of America's most prolific evangelists, Charles Finney, saw no disparity between spiritual regeneration and social reforms. His revivals and antislavery work were never mutually exclusive efforts. He denounced slavery from the pulpit and used his altar calls not only for salvations but also to enlist his converts into the work of abolitionism. He wouldn't allow slaveholders to take communion at his New York churches and considered the destruction of the slave system as a major prerequisite for the coming of the millennium.

We mustn't quarantine Jesus inside our sanctuaries, giving him permission to save souls, while demanding that he leave the affairs of running the world to us! "No one can demand that religion can be relegated to the inner sanctum of personal life," says Pope Francis, "without influencing societal and national life, without concern for the soundness of civil institutions, without a right to offer an opinion on events affecting society."[8]

It's true that the cross is at the core of it all, the crux of his-story. Nevertheless, Jesus came to do more than die. Read the Gospels again and you'll see that he also came to *live* and to show *us* how to live. He came to demonstrate the down-to-earth kingdom that came from heaven. "Jesus doesn't want to be reduced to Secretary of After-life Affairs."[9] He wants to reign over everything and everyone. Here. And now.

---

6. Poplin, *Finding Calcutta*, 33.
7. Jones, *Unshakable Kingdom*, 189.
8. "Pope Francis Urges Bishops," para. 3
9. Greenfield, "No, the Church," para. 22.

Although the Bible is not a manual on social policy, it does offer us principles that structure our moral reasoning, which in turn affects the way we view such things. Jesus teaches us in this discourse (and in others) to integrate his truth into public life with morally compelling and biblically founded convictions.[10]

Imagining the social implications of Christianity doesn't devalue spiritual realities. It means that those realities have social repercussions. Martin Luther King preached that a church that refuses to participate in the struggle for justice will be known as an "institution whose will is atrophied." But if that church will engage in the fight to free itself "from the shackles of a deadening status-quo . . . it will enkindle the imagination of mankind . . . and imbue them with a glowing and ardent love for truth, justice and peace."[11]

The kingdom of heaven insinuates itself on earth to make it more like heaven. "As participants in the civil community," writes Miroslav Volf, "Christians strive to bring it into greater conformity to the character and rule of Christ."[12] Through holy nonconformity, the citizens of the counterintuitive kingdom nudge the social order toward its originally intended form. Our influence reaches beyond getting people to say a "sinner's prayer" and sign up for a new-believers class. Spirit-saturated subversives function, as we'll see later, as "salt" to rescue souls and societies from decay and as "light" to illuminate the path to a better humanity.

Sanctified Subversives

Oscar Romero said that the gospel is "subversive because it does indeed touch the foundations of an order that should not exist, because it is unjust."[13]

Admittedly, the word "subversion" carries a decidedly un-Christian connotation. When I first came across it in a biblical context I recoiled. It felt too aggressive, more *hostile* than *biblical*. But though it normally refers

---

10. The Bible doesn't provide a governing blueprint on every policy or how to legislate our convictions into law. A crystal-clear "Christian" answer to all things political doesn't exist. As we "work out our salvation with fear and trembling," we'll tremble to find discretion and wisdom as we seek to advance God's just kingdom in our own time.

11. King, "Knock at Midnight," para. 11.

12. Volf, *Public Faith in Action*, 7.

13. Romero, *Violence of Love*, 151.

to an attempt to overthrow or undermine a government by working connivingly from within, that's neither the mission of Jesus nor the commission he gave the church. We don't plunder governments or crash cultures. The kingdom we preach works quietly to transform the world one person at a time and one social ill at a time. Our influence isn't derived from wealth, social position, or military power. Instead, it comes from Christian love, prophetic witness, generosity, and sacrificial service.

The Latin origin of the term "subvert" means to "turn from beneath." It usually refers to bringing change from underneath a secretive cover. But Christ's followers influence others from beneath them as servants. He calls us to turn things upside down *from below.*

A South African Dutch clergyman told missionary evangelist E. Stanley Jones: "You preach a very troublesome gospel. We preach a Kingdom in heaven that upsets nothing on earth. You preach a Kingdom of God on earth that upsets everything!" Jones writes: "I would upset everything on one level—the level of this unjust and unworkable world order, to set up everything on the level of a higher order, the Kingdom of God. In watering a dusty road, you have to have to raise a lot of dust in settling it."[14]

It is our mission to partner with God to create a society that more closely reflects Jesus' vision of his kingdom. Our tactics are not to declare war on it, blend into it, or sequester ourselves from it in Christian bunkers. Rather, as Spirit-saturated insurgents we lovingly disrupt the world at its foundations and show our neighbors a better way. "[Our] union with Jesus allows [us] now to be a part of his conspiracy to undermine the structures of evil, which continue to dominate human history, with the forces of truth, freedom, and love."[15]

While we have no right to insist that pre-Christians live like Christians, we must model and recommend what we know to be socially advantageous for the community as a whole. To the exiles in Babylon the Lord said: "Seek the peace and prosperity of the city to which I have carried you into exile. Pray to the Lord for it, because if it prospers, you too will prosper" (Jer 29:7). Their orders were neither to take over Babylon nor isolate themselves from it, but to influence it from within. As we bring our best and seek the best for our generation, everybody wins!

Jesus was a culture-changing, footwashing troublemaker! Instead of royal symbols of sword and chariot he chose a servant's basin and towel.

---

14. Jones, *Song of Ascents*, 105.
15. Willard, *Divine Conspiracy*, 207.

He had all the power of heaven at his disposal, but rather than vaunting himself to dominate, he bent low to wash the feet of those who should've been washing his. He disrupts the top-down system from the bottom up.

He then passes the basin and towel on to us to influence our social order with the same spirit of servanthood. By selfless servitude he subverts the conventional wisdom of the world and requires us to do the same. We don't grope for power, attempt to control reality, or expect the world to understand us, let alone serve us. We love them past their insults and threats and continue to sow seeds of justice and mercy.

"Newness happens in the world," says Walter Brueggemann, "when long silenced people get their voice enough to sing dangerous alternatives."[16]

---

16. Present-day examples of people that have found their voice to sing dangerous alternatives are innumerable. Here are a few that come to mind:
Catholic Charities—https://www.catholiccharitiesusa.org/our-ministry/
WordMadeFlesh—https://wordmadeflesh.org/new-monasticism-new-friars-and-the-third-order-61/
Alongsiders International—https://www.alongsiders.org/
Lutheran Immigration and Refugee Service—https://www.lirs.org/?gclid=Cj0KCQjwjpjkBRDRARIsAKv-oO27IjggfcN9dlVgAxTNlmLlKqHEyGy2ce6B2VLhpsIYtdVKq-plrXVAaAixQEALw_wcB
International Justice Mission—https://www.ijm.org/?gclid=CjoKCQjwjpjkBRDRARIsAKv-oO1Hou83u__Apy-Fs7c9QJQQfqBqBvzWTgTtgeKo1DLryXtkBhIdk-QaAvn-BEALw_wcB
Compassion International—https://www.compassion.com/
Christian Community Development Association—https://ccda.org/
The Simple Way—http://www.thesimpleway.org/
Church of the Savior in Washington D.C.—http://inwardoutward.org/

The Inconvenient Politics of Jesus

The gospel of Jesus Christ is more political than anyone imagines, but in a way that no one guesses.

—Eugene Peterson[1]

He Communicated with Authority

WHEN JESUS FINISHED HIS message that day, Matthew gauged the reaction of his audience and concluded that they "were amazed at his teaching, because he taught as one who had authority, and not as their teachers of the law" (Matt 7:28–29).

Apparently, his crowd was stunned by an inherent "authority," which had nothing to do with the beauty of his oratory or the tone of his delivery. It wasn't bravado or privileged breeding that he brought to the table, or should I say "the hillside."

He was an outsider without noble birth, wealth, specialized religious training, or social standing. Yet he resisted, even challenged imperial Rome's authority, something that their religious experts, who had all of the advantages above, were not willing to do. They were uniformly complicit in Rome's anti-kingdom ways and so forfeited any spiritual authority they had been given by God. As dutiful lackeys of the Empire they taught a watered-down version of Judaism that made no waves among their occupying forces.

Jesus resisted the temptation to derive power through complicity with Rome. Israel's teachers submitted unwaveringly to their occupiers in order to earn their favor. Jesus fearlessly preached a subversive message earning

---

1. Peterson, *Reversed Thunder*, 88.

Rome's disfavor, so they said of him: "We have found this man subverting our nation.... He stirs up the people all over Judea by his teaching."[2]

The message the Jewish leaders preached was *Let's be good Jews and fly under Caesar's radar. We can do our religion in the safety of our synagogues, practice our rituals, and keep our prayers to ourselves. Go along with the program and stay out of trouble.*

Jesus, whose authority came from no less than heaven, produced no such appeals.

He Comported Himself Politically

Dietrich Bonhoeffer wrote: "People say that it is utopian to regard the Sermon on the Mount as a basis for historical-political action.... However, it is not difficult to prove that this view is in conflict with reality."[3]

Though I risk being voted off the island by good sisters and brothers, I'll brave it nonetheless. I believe it's inaccurate to portray Jesus as an apolitical preacher with nothing to say to his socially prejudiced and politically charged context. In fact, he was and is deeply political, but on his own terms with his own priorities that fit no one party. Nevertheless, it could be said that his disruptive agenda is antithetical to the interests of superpowers who rightly see him as a clear and present danger to the status quo which they take (and give) great pains to preserve.

Jesus didn't live or preach in a vacuum. We understand his Sermon best in light of the oppressive context of Rome, staggering taxes, a nearly nonexistent middle class, and rampant race prejudice. This was no cute homily meant to charm the masses, but a mandate designed to do more to disturb the comfortable than comfort the disturbed. And as Catherine Booth, cofounder of the Salvation Army, said, "If we are to better the future we must disturb the present."

He certainly wasn't, in the classic sense, a politician and he only sparingly directly addressed political issues. Instead, he taught and acted in ways that reflected his upside-down kingdom which, rightly understood, informs all of our interactions with the world, including our politics.

We can't allow ourselves, in the interest of separating church from state, to segregate our moral values from public life. "Those Christians who try to avoid all political discussions and engagement are essentially casting

---

2. Luke 23:2, 5.
3. Bonhoeffer, *Cost of Discipleship*, 240.

a vote for the social status quo," says Timothy Keller. "Since no human society reflects God's justice and righteousness perfectly, supposedly apolitical Christians are supporting many things that displease God. So to not be political is to be political."[4]

It's political when we confess that Jesus is Lord and Caesar is not. It is in that sense that the church is a political community that eschews the ways of empire and its emperors. "Finally and fundamentally politics is about justice," writes Peter Wehner, "and justice always matters. You can't be indifferent to politics because politics is about human lives, and if you get your politics wrong there's a huge human cost. And if you get your politics right, you can create the conditions for human flourishing and human dignity."[5]

Though the kingdom can neither be defined by a party or a certain form of government, it most certainly does affect the kind of social convictions we form, policies we support, and politicians we choose to represent us. Among other things, these things matters to God and should therefore matter to us. He didn't set us free from our personal sins so we could keep our social transgressions for ourselves!

Therefore, a good place to begin framing our convictions about such things would be to put ourselves on the hillside along with his spiritually and socially famished audience and listen intently to Jesus' words. What we hear should do more than pique our spiritual interest. It might just overturn some of our notions about how we should conduct ourselves politically.

He Confronted Power Fearlessly

Never did Jesus more daringly confront corruption and greed in both the religion and politics of his day than when he chased money-gouging vendors and their inventory out of his temple, labeling them a "den of thieves and robbers." Both their bad religion and their economically exploitive graft were so repugnant to him that he waged a one-day "Occupy the Temple" protest![6]

By way of exorbitant taxes the priestly nobility raked in extravagant revenue for themselves. Jewish historian of the time, Josephus, deemed

---

4. Keller, *Prodigal Prophet*, 163.
5. Wehner, *Death of Politics*, 126.
6. Since John placed the temple-cleansing episode near the beginning of Jesus' ministry while the Synoptics locate it near the end, some feel that he performed the act twice, indicating that they didn't get the message the first time.

them nothing but a band of avaricious "lovers of luxury." These supposed spiritual leaders formed a class of landowning aristocracy tasked by Rome to extort their fellow citizens and keep order in their communities, a role for which they were dearly compensated.

Jesus strode into the temple and ejected those who forced the faithful to pay a hefty sum to visit God. "The temple clearing was not only a worship corrective but an economic corrective that struck at the heart of a first-century Wall Street."[7]

With one crack of the whip he rebuked corrupt religion that was in cahoots with oppressive government, which marked him a seditious menace in the estimation of both. By this one bold act, Jesus spoke truth to both Roman and Jewish power, which may well have been the final camel's spine-shattering stalk of straw that led to his execution.[8]

Yes, Jesus is political. After the tradition of the prophets, he disrupts injustice where it raises its ugly head and in partnership with his followers, nudges the world toward the Creator's dream for a new social reality. He commissions us to be a people called out of the world, to be the change we want to see in the world. He empowers us to embody a social alternative that the world can't imagine on its own. The question isn't whether or not our faith is political, but rather "*How* is it political?" If and when our faith does intersect with politics it must be on God's terms, not on the terms of the empire.[9]

Now, for the bulk of our study, I invite you to imagine a better world that begins with *attitudes* so radical that we might call them *Utterly Upside-Down Attitudes*.

---

7. Bessenecker, *Overturning Tables*, 13.

8. John Dear wrote: "He did not hit anyone, hurt anyone, kill anyone, or drop any bombs-but he was not passive. He was active, provocative, dangerous, illegal, and civilly disobedient, a disturber of the peace, a troublemaker, a nonviolent revolutionary who broke the unjust laws and mores of an unjust society." Dear, "Civil Disobedience," para. 12.

9. Claiborne and Law, *Jesus for President*, 196.

Part Two

UTTERLY UPSIDE-DOWN ATTITUDES

Even when they call us mad, we know we only preach the subversive witness of the Beatitudes, which have turned everything upside down.
—OSCAR ROMERO

AS ATTITUDES GO, THESE so-called *Beatitudes* are anything but a roundup of the usual suspects. Eugene Peterson nails it in his rendering of them:

> You're blessed:
> ... when you're at the end of your rope
> ... when you feel you've lost what is most dear to you
> ... when you're content with just who you are—no more, no less
> ... when you've worked up a good appetite for God
> ... when you care
> ... when you get your inside world—your mind and heart—put right
> ... when you can show people how to cooperate instead of compete or fight
> ... when your commitment to God provokes persecution.[1]

"The Beatitudes are the moral sublime, the source of awe, the moral purity that takes your breath away and toward which everything points,"

---

1. Peterson, *Message Bible*, 9.

says David Brooks. "In the Beatitudes we see the ultimate road map for our lives."[2]

These eight Blessed Attitudes are so critical that Jesus spends the rest of his Manifesto unpacking them. They summarize the whole Sermon as a sort of "shorthand for what is to come."[3] Possessing and practicing these Christlike qualities propagates everything good that God intends for us. One can hardly imagine a more succinct description of a Jesus-shaped life.

It's best not to view them as independent from the rest of the Discourse like a preface to the body of a lecture. Sometimes when I'm listening to a preacher, I will sort of half listen to the introduction, waiting for the meat of the message. Or when reading a book, I'll impatiently breeze through the preface and flip over to the first chapter. That would be a mistake here as these *blesseds* are not an introduction to the Sermon. Instead, they introduce us *into* the lifestyle that Jesus prescribes throughout the teaching.

Let's imagine these eight attitudes as portals through which we enter, enjoy, and engage with the principles of the rest of the teaching. Each attitude is one of eight doors that lead to a room full of the King's treasures. He begins with them, not in order to warm us up for the message but presents them as doors through which we commence into and practice the message.

If we try to enter the teaching any other way, the best we can expect is to peer over the wall and speculate about what Jesus wants. All we can do is observe it from afar as a lecture about rules to obey instead of as the Christ follower's *rule of life*. We can read his words, analyze them, and dissect them, but we can't live them if we fail to enter through these eight portals.

We can't separate these Beatitudes, as together they portray "a heart whose veins cannot be dissected and pulled to pieces."[4] In order to allay the impression of the attitudes as options from which to choose, like some "Beatitude Buffet," let me morph the metaphor a little. Imagine instead, one big door comprised of all eight as a composite of attitudes that conduct us into the way of Jesus. It's through embodying all eight Beatitudes that we access the rich kingdom life Jesus imagines for us.

Though a few versions translate "blessed" as "happy," I don't think Jesus is referring to a subjective state of happy feelings. It's all too common for many Christians to "fancy the notion of Jesus smiling and providing tips on 'how to be happy,' and would be disappointed should Jesus not give

---

2. Brooks, *Second Mountain*, 245.
3. Moore, *Following the Call*, 3.
4. Arnold, *Salt and Light*, 17.

PART TWO | UTTERLY UPSIDE-DOWN ATTITUDES

us a boost in our very Americanized 'pursuit of happiness.'"[5] The blessings of God actually have precious little to do with how we *feel* about anything. They're much more about how God feels about us. They're about his opinion of us when we exhibit these attitudes. Blessedness is a reflection of the way he engineered us for maximum functionality.

Like a flower, the Sermon unfolds into petals called forgiveness, enemy love, honesty, wholesome sexual ethics, nonviolence, nonreligious spirituality, kingdom economics, equal treatment of all, and the like. The flower is only as beautiful as it is blessed with the attitudes of heart that feed it.

An Intentional Sequence of Attitudes

This is not a salad bar of qualities from which to pick and choose those which appeal to our palate. Neither are they to be compared to the assortment of spiritual gifts that are distributed among us according to divine wisdom. He's not saying that some people are meek, some are merciful, some have pure hearts, and others are simply good at making peace. Instead, he blesses and prescribes *all* these character qualities for *all* people at *all* times.

As such I can't help but imagine an intentional sequence of attitudes, wherein one opens the way to the next. Let me explain.

As we develop a revelation of our own *spiritual poverty* and that of the world, we *mourn* over it, which engenders in us a growing *meekness* before God and others. Discontent to stay that way, we *hunger and thirst* for change. As God gradually and mercifully fills us with the righteousness we seek, we are compelled to show *mercy* to other fellow strugglers. As a result, our hearts embrace fewer conflicting objectives and become increasingly *pure*, which in turn makes us a more quieting influence as *peacemakers*. Finally, when we choose such a culturally preposterous lifestyle, others who live in the opposite way may become aggravated, and *persecute* us for it.

The first three attitudes—*spiritual poverty, mourning, and meekness*—are about emptying ourselves of illusory substitutes for security in possessions, pleasures, and power. This emptying arouses an appetite for a *righteousness* that satisfies our souls. This hunger is the turning point in the list. What follows are the items on his menu for which we ultimately hunger: *mercy, purity, and peacemaking*. And when others observe us living such a way, they may feel compelled to harass us, or worse. We bear their

5. Howell, *Beatitudes for Today*, 15.

persecution as a badge of honor indicating that with God's help we must be doing something right(eous).

See how that works?

Attitudes for Upside-Downers

Rife with paradox, Jesus' "beatitudinal" way catches everyone off guard. Modern-day beatitudes might say something like: "Blessed are the winners of American Idol for they shall see God. Blessed are the first-round draft picks, for they will inherit the earth."[6] Yet Jesus portrays the blessed life where the wealthy are poor and the poor are wealthy, and winners lose while losers end up winning.

Conventional wisdom suggests that this is just not the way the world works. If you live Jesus' way you'll be out of step with the culture that marches to a different beat. Sadly, some of the people with whom you worship every Sunday will protest the loudest.

In a culture that thrives on success and strength, anti–Beatitudes might sound a little like this: *Blessed are the middle class in spirit, those who cause others to mourn, who are at work to prove their superiority over others, who take advantage of the vulnerable, who show no mercy, whose hearts are divided, who make war, and who persecute others for their own righteousness sake.*

His terms like *poverty, mourning, meekness, hunger, thirsting, mercy, and persecution* all suggest vulnerability—weakness if you will. Not surprising, since Jesus is nothing if not a King that chose to make his entrance here as needy and weak. Born in a barn, raised in relative poverty, homeless as an adult, rode a donkey to his procession into the capital city, slain on a criminal's cross, and buried in a borrowed cave.

These Christlike qualities don't tend to appear on self-help seminar brochures like these:

> *The Power of Now*
>
> *How to Stop Doubting Your Greatness*
>
> *Ten Keys to Unlimited Power*
>
> *The Magic of Thinking Big*
>
> *The New Science of Personal Achievement*

6. Suttle, *Evangelical Social Gospel*, 37.

PART TWO | UTTERLY UPSIDE-DOWN ATTITUDES

"What is prized by human beings," Jesus says, "is an abomination in the sight of God" (Luke 16:15). It becomes clear that the qualities he prizes are scandalous to modern sensibilities. From an encounter with earthlings a visitor from space might return with a description of our anti-Beatitudes: "Blessed are the bombastic, bellicose, and bloodthirsty." By contrast, Jesus' behavior was so outside the box that even his own family thought he was crazy (Mark 3:21)! If you choose to follow in his steps your friends and family may well arrive at a similar conclusion about you.

Ronnie McBrayer says, "We must embrace and take hold of these apparent weaknesses, clinging to them as the very places where Christ will enter, reveal himself, and rebuild our lives with blessedness."[7]

Serendipitous Consequences

Each of these characteristics has an inherent consequence. "Theirs is the Kingdom," he says of the poor in spirit. Mourners will be "comforted," the pure in heart will "see God," peacemakers will bear such a resemblance to God that they'll be known as his children, and so on.

Rather than blessings to chase after, I consider these as *serendipitous consequences*. I don't think Jesus is suggesting that we act a certain way in order to achieve a certain result. In such case God would act as our personal vending machine. We make our selection, put in the right change, and out comes the blessing. We do (A), he therefore owes us (B). This sort of paradigm is *transactional* rather than relational. And last I checked, he's a relational God.

He's not implying, "Try to be poor in spirit so you can get the Kingdom," or "Mourn in order to be comforted," or "Show mercy so God will be merciful to you." The Beatitudes are not a prescription for how to be blessed as much as a *description* of who is. In other words, regardless of which direction the cultural wind is blowing, this is the life that God calls "blessed."

Attitudes We Ought To Be Havin'

Notice these are "BE-attitudes." He's talking about *being* a certain way, which is quite different than *doing* certain things. Okay, that's a bit of a

7. McBrayer, *Jesus Tribe*, 46.

PART TWO | UTTERLY UPSIDE-DOWN ATTITUDES

lexical stretch, but you get my point. In each case he says, "Blessed are those who *are* . . ." this way or that. The attitudes are more about *being* than *doing* and the blessings attached to them are more about what God thinks than how we feel.

This is not to say that these Christlike *attitudes* don't inevitably result in Christlike *actions,* because they absolutely do. But, as we've seen, attempting Christlike-ness from the outside in quickly turns to a sweaty spirituality, which is pretty unpleasant for both the one who sweats and those among whom he sweats, if you get my drift!

We must view them less as demands on us and more as descriptions of the values of kingdom persons. Rather than using these as a spiritual to-do list, I advise us to embrace them as an invitation into the characteristics of those who live christianly. "To say (for instance) that the peacemakers are those who flourish is an observation, not a demand that one become a peacemaker. On the other hand, it implies that becoming a peacemaker is a good idea if one wants to flourish."[8]

I wonder if the metric that Jesus uses here could in some circles be described as "un-American." "God seems to bless the very antithesis of many of the things America has come to stand for: prosperity, pride, and power," says Mark Labberton."[9] As much as I love my country, I believe that we've sunk quite a distance from the nation that some people once called "Christian." These attitudes, nearly nonexistent in the culture, not to mention in short supply in the American church, are especially critical in these times.

The Political Connection

In our democratic republic we have the privilege of electing candidates that have the best chance of moving the nation in at least the general direction of God's design. While we don't expect our public servants, especially those who don't profess faith in Christ, to act like Christians, there is an irreducible modicum of morality that we would be wise to expect from them. Since most of their legislative decisions have moral implications, we must, in good conscience, support those candidates whose values are most aligned with Christ's and whose policies benefit the common good and not just our own personal agendas.

8. Eklund, *Beatitudes through the Ages,* 62.
9. Labberton, *Still Evangelical,* 168.

PART TWO | UTTERLY UPSIDE-DOWN ATTITUDES

What is most disturbing to me is the large percentage of so-called Christians who seem to subordinate their faith to partisan loyalties and political power. They view God through the lens of their party's platform rather than the other way around. They support and defend amoral candidates and vote for policies that are antithetical to the teachings of Jesus, especially the Sermon on the Mount.[10]

If we want a better world for ourselves and for our children we must be better practitioners of our faith. This is why we must look long and hard at these radical ways of Jesus' kingship until they become deeply imbedded in our hearts.

We'll unpack each "blessed" in hopes that our hearts will be sufficiently supple for the Spirit to massage them into our souls.

So Here's the Plan

Each of these *attitudes that we ought to be havin'* leads to specific *actions that we ought to be livin'*. That is, Beatitudes breed behavior. Character causes conduct.

Jesus spends the body of his address applying these eight qualities to real-life situations. So rather than walking through Matt 5–7 verse by verse like a commentator would, we'll unfurl each Beatitude by introducing slices of the Sermon that reflect the value of each one. As we do, we'll focus our attention on the moral imperatives with social implications.

It might be helpful to hear it as a song rather than read it as a sermon. Think of it in musical terms wherein the Beatitudes serve as the refrain and the rest of the lyrics as stanzas in Jesus' *Ballad to Believers*.

They say that a story is only as good as its author and a sermon is only as good as its preacher. Let us not separate the Sermonizer from the Sermon. "This Sermon is vascular. Cut it anywhere and it will bleed Jesus."[11]

---

10. This is not exclusive to one party. Both sides of the aisle in US politics support anti-kingdom politicians and policies.

11. Jones, *Unshakable Kingdom*, 239.

Part Two | Utterly Upside-Down Attitudes

So put yourself on the grass before him, smell the mountainside flora, picture his visage, and as he speaks (or sings), hear his voice appealing to you and to me to live *his way*. Ask him to pause once in a while as you ponder his meaning—and yours.

Blessed Are the Broken

Blessed are the poor in spirit for theirs is the Kingdom of heaven.
—MATT 5:3

God cannot fill what is full. He can fill only emptiness—deep poverty. It is not how much we really "have" to give—but how empty we are—so that we can receive fully in our life and let him live his life in us. Take away your eyes from yourself and rejoice that you have nothing.
—MOTHER TERESA

NOT EXACTLY THE HEADLINE you'd expect from the greatest Sermon ever preached. Right out of the gate Jesus displays his unnerving knack for disorienting our calcified approach to spirituality. I figure this would've put some of his listeners, especially the most sanctimonious, on their back foot. I doubt this would have ended up on a flyer advertising their *Religion 101 Class*.

Reminds me of the first of AA's Twelve Steps: "We admitted we were powerless over alcohol—that our lives had become unmanageable." The Twelve Steps and the Beatitudes have an uncanny similarity. They both address the destitute and leave no viable recourse but to run to a "power greater than ourselves to restore us to sanity."

Everything Jesus teaches here, and everywhere else for that matter, targets those people who are aware that they're spiritually incompetent. It is not perfection but the conviction of imperfection that leads to salvation. He might as well have said: *Blessed are ones who are convinced they can't live the way God wants them to live in their own power.*

Part Two | Utterly Upside-Down Attitudes

The poor in spirit "remember they are dust"—beloved dust.[1] Only when we're aware of our own helplessness can God help us, and consequently help us help other helpless people.

Blessed are the desperate. That's the message here. Thomas Merton says, "If we were incapable of humility, we would be incapable of joy, because humility alone can destroy the self-centeredness that makes joy impossible."[2]

If you are poor in spirit, the kingdom and its blessings are available to you because of—not in spite of—your spiritual poverty. Martin Luther once commented that this is the first Beatitude because, even if one feels spiritually rich at the beginning of the Sermon, one will feel terribly poor and needy by the end! So, if you're not sufficiently desperate I recommend that you take an honest and introspective stroll through the rest of the text and see how you fare. If you're not desperate by the end, pray that you will be soon, and read it again.

The narcissist has no redemptive influence on a culture that is already obsessed with itself. He can't fit others into his heart because it's already full of himself. He has fabricated his own role in life to write, produce, direct, and star in his own autobiographical docudrama. He only reaches out to others when he needs "extras" to make him look good by appearing in the background and mouthing the lines he gives them.

On the other hand, those who concede their deficiency tend to be the best consensus-builders. They know what they're made of and treat others with modesty. Like all good servants, willing to subordinate their own desires, they devote themselves to making *other people* successful. Rather than disadvantage the community to advantage themselves, the poor in spirit are willing to disadvantage themselves in order to advantage others.

I was surprised to see that in the Microsoft Word ecosystem the term "servanthood" is a non-word. When you type it, the red wobbly underline appears indicating that you've made a mistake. Evidently, to their in-house dictionary, "servanthood" is a typo!

"Motherhood, brotherhood, manhood, likelihood, knighthood, even babyhood don't get flagged as misspelled. But *servanthood* has no place in the English language."[3] This should be no surprise in a culture whose chief

---

1. Ps 103:14.
2. Merton, *New Seeds of Contemplation*, 52.
3. Bessenecker, *How to Inherit the Earth*, 49.

premise is competition for the top rung. You don't hear many kids say they want to be a "servant" when they grow up!

In contrast, the term Jesus uses here for the "poor" is the one they used in his day to describe people at the very bottom end of the socioeconomic ladder, the exceedingly destitute. It literally refers to people so poor they are "bent over." The poor in spirit are in a constant state of bowing. Since crowns don't come with chinstraps, we can't very well bend over to bow at Jesus' feet without our crowns falling off our head!

"Give God thanks for every weakness, fault, and imperfection you have," says Jeremy Taylor. "Accept it as a favor of God, an instrument to resist pride and nurse humility."[4] To a social order that worships strength and decries weakness, where the rich and famous loom over the poor and obscure, this notion of spiritual poverty is utterly nonsensical.

The posture of what we might call the "middle-class in spirit" dominates American secular culture and surprisingly thrives also in the ranks of prosperity-clamoring Christendom. Our proud hearts, so complicit with the conceited spirit of the age, dull our ability to accept the benevolent kingship of Jesus into our hearts, let alone advance it in the world.

To the self-satisfied Laodiceans Jesus says, "You say, 'I am rich; I have acquired wealth and do not need a thing.' But you do not realize that you are wretched, pitiful, poor, blind and naked" (Rev 3:17). The good church folk of Laodicea left Jesus outside on the stoop knocking on the church door, calling out to get in (Rev 3:20). I'm afraid that this is the predicament of much of the Western Church today. We've been co-opted by the triumphalist and consumerist vision of the American Dream where our services and seminars sound more like Amway rallies than the fellowship of the spiritually impoverished.

The social implications of this Beatitude are countless. How can we claim to bring hope to the world if the hope we possess runs only as deep as our own fallen faculties? The paternalistic "middle-class in spirit" Christian claims more than is his. *I'm right and you're wrong, I'm strong and you're weak. I'm rich and you're poor. I'm good and you're bad!*

Not really the most inviting message.

Spiritual poverty is a universal problem. Our pedigrees and portfolios may differ but we're all the same beneath the epidermis. "All have sinned and fall short of the glory of God." While you may not come up as short as I

---

4. Foster, *Devotional Classics*, 247.

do, you still miss the mark. We can never hit the target no matter how many times we shoot at it.

Until we recognize our common moral disease, the chasm between classes, races, parties, and nations will only widen. The seventh Beatitude, the one about *peacemakers*, is intrinsically rooted in this first one. Only those who admit their own limitations can make peace with God, with others, and among others.

Ronnie McBrayer tells a story about the famous G. K. Chesterton:

> When Chesterton was at his peak of popularity and wit, the *London Times* solicited responses from its readership by asking the question: "What is wrong with the world?" You can imagine the result. Hundreds of long, detailed letters poured in to the editor. Then *The Times* asked a number of leading thinkers of the day to respond with full essays answering the question. Again, the essays poured in, verbose and long-winded. The shortest and most powerful response came from Chesterton. Here is his answer to what is wrong with the world. He wrote, "Dear Sirs, I am. Yours truly, G. K. Chesterton."

Ironically, the "surpassing righteousness"[5] into which Jesus summons us is only remotely possible for those who admit their scarcity of anything approximating righteousness. Spiritual experts concoct a faux righteousness of their own. The genuine article, on the other hand, is created in heaven and then activated by grace inside willing recipients. Manmade righteousness is *achieved* by hard work and grit while the God kind is *received* by means of an honest admission of neediness. "The knowledge of our own poverty brings us to the moral frontier where Jesus Christ works."[6]

Furthermore, deny our destitution and we lose our "saltiness"[7] with which to purge out evil and preserve goodness in the earth. In order to solve disputes without rage,[8] treat women with respect,[9] tell the truth[10] even when it isn't popular, refrain from revenge,[11] and love those who hate us,[12]

---

5. Matt 5:20.
6. Chambers, *My Utmost for His Highest*, 211.
7. Matt 5:13.
8. Matt 5:22.
9. Matt 5:28.
10. Matt 5:37.
11. Matt 5:39.
12. Matt 5:44.

we have to begin with a zero balance in our moral account. It all starts with poverty.

The words of moral superiors, who speak in the heat of the moment rather than from the heart of God, tend to "fall to the ground"[13] before they arrive at their intended target—and thankfully so. Therefore, beware of arrogant, angry prophets.

> People who are in the right are usually in the greatest danger of being a nuisance. The fact that they are right, and know it, has a powerful tendency to make them intolerant with those who were not in a position to see it their way. And this further alienates people. Truth is most often hurt by its own advocates.[14]

On the other hand, patient peacefulness is a virtue that grows out of poverty of spirit and is indispensable for culture-disrupters who speak truth to power.

By nature, we're all running on empty and can only "do justly" or "love mercy" by first "walking humbly" with God (Mic 6:8).

Jesus begins his Manifesto with what might be his most counterintuitive announcement. The kingship that God wields in heaven makes its way to earth through people poor enough in spirit to receive it, live in it, and advance it. Those who do so are "blessed."[15]

---

13. 1 Sam 3:19.

14. Jordan, *Sermon on the Mount*, 31.

15. For each Beatitude I'll suggest one historical figure that embodied that Kingdom characteristic particularly well. For "poor in spirit" I commend to you the great missionary, David Brainerd and his autobiography, *The Life and Diary of David Brainerd*.

The Groan of the Godly

Blessed are those who mourn for they shall be comforted.

—Matt 5:4

There is a time . . . to weep, and a time to laugh; a time to mourn, and a time to dance.

—Eccl 3:4

Jesus' ancestors and contemporaries knew how to face their sufferings in such a way as to give themselves the best chance of receiving divine comfort. They dumped ashes on their heads, ripped a hole in their shirt, sat on the ground, and wept. Hard on the clothes but good for the soul.

Lament is an indispensable periodic posture for the person who loves Jesus and loves the same people he loves. Those who do it are "comforted" by the fact that they are loving people in the way Jesus loves them and are therefore those whom God deems "blessed."

I love to worship God joyfully both in private and in public. Aligning myself with heaven in worship does me good, transforms the spiritual atmosphere around me, and readies me to hear God's whisper and then do what he says. I also believe that if praise brings heaven's power to earth, heartfelt lament brings earth's pain before heaven. The Lord's ear is tuned to the collective "ouch!" of his people. He hears our "groans" (Exod 6:5).

Mourning is not exactly a hot topic in the church universe today. I don't expect to see book titles such as *Weeping Worshippers* or *Learning the Art of Lament* topping the charts on Amazon. If you want a crowd, publicize a seminar on *Seven Steps to Success* or *Ten Keys to Joy*. But *How to*

The Groan of the Godly

Mourn or *Grieving God's Way* wouldn't garner enough signups to pay for the hall!

As always, Jesus makes no effort to fit himself inside peoples' preferences. He starts out by calling us to concede our poverty and then to grieve it, neither of which would we naturally think of as beelines to blessedness. Even so it's the "broken spirit and contrite heart" that he values above all.[1]

True mourners, the ones who choose to care until it hurts, are described by *blessedness* and are candidates for "comfort." On the contrary the most miserable people tend to be those who shun the cares of others in the interest of their own happiness. In their efforts to save their lives they "lose" them.[2]

Not all tears are created equal. They come in an assortment of patterns and in response to a variety of circumstances. There are attention-getting tears and tears of self-pity. I've cried enough of both of those myself to know that they don't yield anything good. Then there are tears of repentance and others of joy. I recommend both of those at their appropriate times.

Other good tears are shed in grief, uncertainty, confusion, fear, and empathy. In the biblical narrative, poets, prophets, and apostles all shed and recommend these kinds of tears as both personally therapeutic and socially potent. "Our tears are sacred. They water the ground around our feet so new things can grow."[3]

Given the chaos and suffering in the world it is disrespectful to our fellow sufferers and to the God who suffers with us to plaster permanent Pollyanna grins on our faces. While it's true that "Weeping may endure for the night, but joy comes in the morning," we don't know when morning will come. We simply can't afford to hasten past grief while waiting for the sun to make its appearance.

"The groan is the vernacular of pain," says Max Lucado, "the chosen tongue of despair. When there are no words, these are the words. When prayer won't come, these will have to do. Sunnier times hear nicer, more poetic petitions, but stormy times generate mournful sounds of sadness, fear, and dread."[4]

---

1. Ps 51:17.
2. Matt 10:39.
3. Bell and Golden, *Jesus Wants to Save Christians*, 44.
4. McNeel, "Grieving Our Broken Border," para. 14.

The Collective "Ouch!"

Ah, how Thy grace hath wooed my soul
With persevering wiles!
Now give me tears to weep; for tears
Are deeper joy than smiles.

—Frederick William Faber

Those who have not cared enough to grieve will not know joy.
—Walter Brueggemann[1]

A little boy threw his uneaten half sandwich in the trashcan when his mother told him, "God cries when you waste food."

"I don't hear anything," he said.

"It's because you're not listening!" she replied.

Whether over wasted food or wasted lives, if we can't hear God cry it's because we're not listening. And if we can't hear him weep and join in a collective cry with him and his friends, we're missing out on the blessedness and comfort that he promises.

Mourning is a sort of "Ouch!" that we blurt out for our own brokenness and the brokenness of others. It's the sorrow we experience when we recognize the loss of what's good in our collective human nature. Grief, says John Dear, "is a spiritual practice that opens us to the anguish of those around the world affected by war, violence, and poverty."[2]

---

1. Brueggemann, *Prophetic Imagination*, 118.
2. Dear, *Beatitudes of Peace*, 51.

Did you know that *apathy* doesn't mean we don't *care*? It means we don't *feel*. Its opposite is *empathy*, which means we share in others' feelings and "mourn with those who mourn."[3] Bonhoeffer used to tell his students that one could only rejoice in Christ if they wept with the Jewish community in their suffering under the Nazis.

Mourners mourn for their own sin and suffering and join in the collective "ouch" of their neighbors, the ones nearby as well as those far away. Our mourning is not adequately framed as we lament our own individual brokenness, but includes identifying with our fellow sinners. How else can we respond with spiritual and emotional integrity to the misrule of God's world by the devil's agents, to starving children, genocide, terrorism, and moral dysphoria? It's part of our prophetic role to grieve while confronting the conscience of society.

Weeping is only the first step toward the advance of God's justice in the earth but it's a start. Shane Claiborne says, "When we ask God to move a mountain, God may give us a shovel." Lamenting actually helps us locate the shovel. It's where we begin to care enough to do something about the mountains that need leveling and the gardens that need planting. "Those who go out weeping, carrying seed to sow, will return with songs of joy, carrying sheaves with them" (Ps 126:6). The best weepers are doers—shovel-carrying weed-whacking seed sowers.

Jesus neither instructs us to drown in our sorrows in perpetual melancholy nor to drown our sorrows in the intoxicants of happy thoughts and positive confessions. Many, while failing to weep with the Father over his broken beloveds, buoy themselves by singing victory choruses and filling their pockets with *promise box* verses. But bone-crushing poverty, human trafficking, school shootings, and senseless wars over money and power beg us to cry "Ouch!"

I remember the Sunday following one of our country's many mass shootings in which fifteen people lost their lives and many were wounded. I went to church hoping for an opportunity to shed some tears with brothers and sisters and pray for the survivors, but all we did was sing snappy songs, listen to a sermon on how to be prosperous, and pray for our own pay raises. I left that service with yet another tragedy to mourn on my own.

---

3. Rom 12:15.

PART TWO | UTTERLY UPSIDE-DOWN ATTITUDES

Does it not seem reasonable that Christians would be those most likely to be sensitized to our own sad spiritual state and the state of the world? Are these realities not sufficient to elicit mournful tears—a sort of *holy sorrow*?[4]

If you're having a hard time identifying things worthy of lament all you have to do is to notice how far we've drifted from Jesus' standard of personal and social righteousness that he speaks to in this address.

Let's peruse some of his Sermon's main points, identify how far we've fallen from kingdom values, and let us mourn.

While He Calls for Love and Forgiveness, Our World is Increasingly Angry and Vengeful. Ouch!

We bleat and bellow against the other party, the other ethnicity, the other socioeconomic class, the other gender, and all the *other others!* Since murder is birthed in the womb of nurtured anger,[5] how can we hide our heads in our hymnbooks and fail to grieve the most recent mass shooting, hate crime, or suicide bombing? What would it look like for a church that sings exclusively happy songs to "leave our gift at the altar"[6] and take a moment to mourn our society's divisions and dysphoria?

---

4. Even King David, maybe best known for his happy praise songs, along with his lyricist cohorts, was big on lamenting. Psalms, the Bible's longest book, devotes huge chunks of its poetry to the expression of sadness over the human condition:
I am worn out from groaning; *all night long I flood my bed with* weeping *and drench my couch with* tears. *My eyes grow weak with* sorrow; *they fail because of all my foes.*
I am feeble and utterly crushed; I groan in anguish of heart.
My thoughts trouble me and I am distraught.
How long must I wrestle with my thoughts and every day have sorrow *in my heart? How long will my enemy triumph over me?*
My heart is in anguish within me; the terrors of death assail me.

5. Matt 5:21.

6. Matt 5:23.

No Doubt Our Derisive Name-Calling and Derogatory Labeling[7] of Fellow Image-Bearers Breaks the Heart of the Father. Ouch!

Pejorative propagandizing soars from mouths to ears like a virus sickening anyone who inhales it. No one is immune to this highly infectious airborne disease. Breathing through the filter of Jesus' life and teaching is the only cure for the infection.

The most efficient way to sling mud is to do it with a broad brush. The broader the brush the greater volume of mud is slung! One universally favored broad brush is name-calling. It saves a lot of time and verbiage to just call someone a derogatory name.

Though we've come to expect this sort of immature behavior from media shock jocks and politicians (some more than others), there's no excuse for supposed followers of Jesus to engage in such libelous labeling! Since we can't praise God with our mouth and turn around to "curse human beings, who have been made in God's likeness," our speech must be "full of grace, seasoned with salt." (Jas 3:9; Col 4:6).

It Broke His Heart to Speak to the Lust in our Hearts, Adultery in Our Marriages, and a Culture of Divorce.[8] Ouch!

"There are two kids in the bushes right outside having sex!" shouted Steve, rushing into the church office shocked and breathless.

Our church facilities were located adjacent to a high school campus. Hundreds of students passed through our property every day on their way home. Some lingered on our lawn before, during, and after school. This we loved for the many opportunities it afforded us to befriend those young souls. The most common inconveniences we experienced were relentless graffiti on our walls, clouds of pot smoke wafting into the office windows, and the occasional brawl in the parking lot. Copulating in the bushes was a whole other level of disruption of our daily office routine!

As shocked as I was about the situation, what took me most by surprise was my initial visceral reaction. When we arrived outside to confront the kids, who had already fled the scene of the crime, I stood there and cried.

7. Matt 5:22.
8. Matt 5:27–32.

All I could think of was how sad it was that two children could've possessed such a damaged moral compass that in broad daylight right next to a place of worship they could trample their innocence. How tragic that anyone of any age could become that estranged from God and indifferent to his healthy, holy ways! All I could do was stand there and weep.

Sure, eventually I got angry, but not so much with the kids themselves, but with the complicity between sin, Satan, and the system of this world that so thoroughly corrupts young minds (and a lot of old ones too). We went on to report it to the campus police, which is grievous in itself that schools need police in the first place! But my first reaction was tears.

Jesus Speaks the Truth[9] and Is the Truth Speaking, Yet From the Highest Level on Down, Ours Is a "Post-Truth" Culture. That Deserves a Huge Ouch!

Speechwriter for several US presidents Peter Wehner said: "When some large number of the people in a country buy into this [post-truth narrative]—if they make up their own narrative—then a society begins to fracture in the deepest way. That is what is going on . . . day after day after day, and it's taking a terrific toll—a political toll, and a civic toll, and a social toll."

Most disturbing to me is the preponderance of those who identify as "Christian" who seem to be unfazed by the *truth decay* that is rotting our social order from the inside out. Of all people, shouldn't we who claim to follow "The Truth" (John 14:6) be first in line to tell the truth and mourn the culture of lies that shatters social *shalom*?

Jesus Demands Enemy Love and Nonviolent Resistance[10] While Hostility and Violence Flourish Here and Abroad. Ouch!

We'll unpack his eye-for-an-eye, cheek-turning love of enemies more fully later. Suffice it to say that our cutthroat culture has a long way to go to approximate his kingdom ethic. Problem is, the same could be said of the church, which often seems to glean a triumphalist demeanor from the

---

9. Matt 5:37.
10. Matt 5:38–43.

pages of the Old Testament rather than from the the New, wherein Jesus flipped the script. While God signed off on conquering nations in order to protect his investment in national Israel until Messiah arrived, newsflash: he arrived! And he clearly changed the narrative from killing our enemies to loving them.

A missionary friend of mine in Israel told me about the only two Christian churches in his small town that were at such odds with each other that they exchanged death threats between them. Ouch!

The Pharisees Are the Same Yesterday, Today, and Forever! Ouch!

> Don't make a performance out of it. It might be good theater, but the God who made you won't be applauding. (Matt 6:1, The Message)

Giving, praying, fasting, and the like, unless practiced from an empathetic heart before an audience of One is simply empty religion—faux spirituality. This, we must mourn.

It's Impossible to Serve the True God and the False God Called "Mammon"[11] at the Same Time, Yet We Keep Trying to Do Just That. Ouch!

Instead of mourning money-madness we imbibe in its intoxication. To our shame, instead of modeling the simple life into which Jesus summons us, we jump on the same *Prosperity-Now* train whose passengers careen toward a washed-out bridge.

We reason that our best marketing strategy is to impress pre-Christians with a religion of accumulation wherein we promise them God-generated success: *If you possess as much faith as ours, pray with the formula that we give you, attend our church, and give your 10 percent, you too can be healthy, wealthy, and rise to the skies!* Ouch!

Is it possible that people are looking for a community that knows how to grieve its forfeitures and how to bring their sorrows to Someone bigger than themselves for comfort? Could it be that they're longing for a

---

11. Matt 6:24.

place where people engage in the pains of the world rather than hide their heads in the sham of spiritual sand while claiming their diamond-studded destiny?

His Pièce de Résistance, the So-Called "Golden Rule,"[12] Sounds Like a Pipe Dream to Our Self-Indulgent, Racially Divided, Nationalistic, Consumeristic Consciences. Ouch!

"Treat people like you want them to treat you." Pretty simple, really. I said "simple," not *easy*. But don't you know that if this were the grid through which we processed all our choices, we would already be enjoying heaven's kingdom on earth? Sadly though, we use an altogether dysfunctional grid, the *me-first grid*.

Can I get an *"Ouch"* for all this?

---

12. Matthew 7:12

The "Ouchless" Church

Grieve, mourn and wail. Change your laughter to mourning and your joy to gloom.

—Jas 4:9

The future is given to those who are experienced in groaning.

—Walter Brueggemann[1]

Picture this. You have nine siblings. Four of them live in abject poverty, two of which are dying of a treatable disease. Two others are drug-dealing murderous gangsters. Another two are healthy, wealthy, yet not wise. They live hedonistically, and have no spiritual inclination or social compassion. The last one, along with you, is a devoted follower of Jesus. You and she love God with all your hearts and your neighbors as yourselves.

The question is, how can you be anything but heartbroken over your other siblings' sins and sufferings? To be lost in your own pursuit of happiness and spiritual blessing, and yet fail to mourn their lack thereof, is nothing but un-Christian.

If being in sync with God includes mourning anything that's out of sync with him, why are so many of us so reluctant to do it? Are we resistant or simply oblivious? Why are so many in the contemporary church so "ouchless"?

---

1. Brueggemann, *Prophetic Imagination*, 110.

Addicted to Positivity

In my opinion, as we try to keep our churches on an upbeat trajectory, we bypass an important leg of the journey. We rush too quickly to joy when there is so much to lament along the way. Of course, the Bible teaches us to rejoice in spite of our sufferings, but this doesn't map out our entire itinerary toward ultimate triumph. We're permitted, even commanded, to take brief (if not prolonged) detours into lament when warranted.

Many Christians typically try to pray away sin and suffering and dodge the essential stage of mourning it. Enamored with spiritual highs, they treat sadness like it's a sickness and work to rid themselves of it as quickly as possible.

Mourning our convoluted culture serves as labor pains that ultimately result in new life. "I wanted faith to work like an epidural; to numb the pain of vulnerability," writes Brené Brown. "As it turned out, my faith ended up being more like a midwife—a nurturing partner who leans into the discomfort with me and whispers 'push' and 'breathe.'"

A Flimsy Theology

"Everything that happens is sovereignly ordained by God." Is that true?

If it's all part of his plan, then the Holocaust, September 11th, and the genocide in Yemen were ordained and are therefore unworthy of being mourned. Then all despots and corrupt politicians occupy the offices eternally ordained for them. Then every baby born with severe disabilities and every woman raped is part of God's blueprint, and therefore mourning has no place among the faithful.

No, these are things to mourn, not explain.

Bad theology circumvents good practice, including the practice of the kind of mourning that Jesus claims has a *blessed* quality to it.

What Good Does it Do?

Mourning is a waste of time. We have a world to win, so why should we spend our time lamenting? I understand the sentiment. But is it actually a waste of time?

As counterintuitive as it sounds, mourners are visionaries. Prophetic lament includes hope in its repertoire. D. L. Mayfield says that lament is "a sign of radical hope in a God who is listening. It is people feeling close enough to God to pour forth what is in their hearts and people trusting God enough to believe that another world might be possible."[2]

Pulpits topped with sweat and spit from angry preachers ranting against all the evildoers in the world don't compare in eternal value with podiums washed in the tears of compassionate messengers. The former reeks of self-righteous certitude, which gives preacher and audience a false sense of chest-pumping power, while the latter exposes a true vulnerability and exhibits a sense of dependent powerlessness.

Full disclosure, given the choice, I'll go for certainty over vulnerability any day. But Jesus begins with poverty and proceeds to mourning, which ultimately leads to a fuller access to the blessedness of his kingship. Without the prerequisite mourning, our hope tends to attach itself to human ingenuity rather than to *the God of hope.*

First, we mourn what is broken, then we place our hope in the Repairer of broken things. "He turns our mourning into dancing" (Ps 31:10). Until we've mourned, we may dance, but not necessarily with him!

Self-Absorption

Grieving our personal losses like deaths of loved ones, marriage breakups, health crises, etc., is not only legitimate, it's an important prescription for emotional health. Nevertheless, it's the "Ouch!" on behalf of others that we seem to, more often than not, skip over. Failing to grieve the losses of others is not only unhealthy, it's inhumane. It's this greater collective "Ouch!" that we must recover in the church if we're going to be blessed and be a blessing.

Oh, and by the way, when you mourn, don't mourn alone.

---

2. Mayfield, *Myth of the American Dream*, 131.

See You in the Mourning

Mourn with those who mourn.
—Rom 12:15

Our tears are all the emotions for which we do not have words.
—Yolanda Pierce[1]

Weep With Other Weepers

THE SORT OF REDEMPTIVE mourning Jesus calls *blessed* is best done on behalf of and in the company of other mourners.

As a pastor, I witnessed a lot of heartbreaking situations, nevertheless I wasn't really able to internalize the kind of pain that fills the human heart until I experienced a bit of it myself. Mourning the loss of my marriage (to divorce) and my health (to cancer) schooled me in grieving the sin and suffering of others whose suffering was greater than my own. Spending quality time with other sufferers—especially hopeless houseless folk—also increases my capacity for grieving the losses of others. Listening to their stories of abuse and abandonment sensitizes my soul to their pain and primes the pump for tears to flow.

Though our destitution may not be obvious at first glance, we're all soul-broken, cracked, and leaking humans. Loss is a lesson the Master Teacher uses to remind us of our universal poverty. Unfortunately, only some of us learn her lessons and pass her tests. As we lean into what she

---

1. Yolanda Pierce is Dean of the Howard University School of Divinity. She tweeted this after officer Derek Chauvin's murder conviction of George Floyd.

teaches us, divine compassion seeps into our souls and trickles back out to others through the cracks created by hard blows.

Our tears flow from a place of connectivity and complicity with the world's corruption. We may be citizens of heaven but we live on earth and are laden with the same proclivities that disappoint our Lord and harm his people. As did the prophets,[2] we must confess our solidarity with fellow sinners and saints and repent alongside them.

As members of the same broken humanity, others' sins are *our* sins. Therefore, we weep. As saved-but-not-yet-sinless people we repent of things we may not have personally perpetrated, yet we bear the burden of them in solidarity with our fellow humans. We lament and repent of our shared sinfulness.

The best way to learn to love our enemies is to first pray for them. It's hard to imagine interceding for others without first putting ourselves in their shoes. Intercessory prayer often requires weeping with other weepers, particularly with those who don't know how to pray or weep for themselves.

Compassion is where we so intently identify with others' pain that it finds its way into our hearts and leads the way to intercession. The two are symbiotic. The former incites the latter, at which time the tables turn and the latter increases the former.

Eugene H. Peterson said: "[Jeremiah] hurt because he cared.... He felt in his own being all the aching hurt of unrequited love. Having identified so thoroughly with God's message, he also felt the rejection in every bone and muscle. Their blasphemies cut him; their clumsy rebellions bruised him; their thoughtless rituals salted his open wounds."[3]

I have to admit, sometimes when I pray for people who hurt other people, I'm like Jonah who had no interest in the salvation of the Ninevites. Yet, if the alternative involves being swallowed up by a big fish, the least I can do is pray!

God hates sin for the harm it does to the people he loves. Being compassionate toward other sinners doesn't require that we downplay their culpability. But I do find it easier to show love and mercy to people by putting the wreckage of their lives in the context of our shared humanity.

William Booth, the founder of the Salvation Army, often paced the floor in the middle of the night. On one such night his son found him and asked him what he was doing. "Ah, Bramwell," he said, "I'm thinking about

---

2. Dan 9:4–20.
3. Peterson, *Run With the Horses*, 100.

the people's sin. What will people do with their sin?" Jesus was thinking about our sin when he chose to share in our humanness, die as though complicit in our sinfulness, and pray for our forgiveness!

We mustn't mourn alone, but in solidarity with other mourners. Wait, there's more . . .

Weep with the Weeper of Heaven

Are you sad about what's wrong with the world? You're in good company. Before he judges, God weeps and invites us to weep with him.

Join in the grief of the *Weeper of Heaven*. Weep, not only with other weepers, but also in the company of him who weeps over the wreckage of the world he loves. How far we are from the Creator's intended ideal when we leave him to weep alone!

Over sin, sickness, and suffering Jesus wept,[4] the Spirit grieves,[5] and the Father aches.[6] Intimacy with God includes feeling what he feels. In lament we press into his heart and partner with him to do what we can to repair what is broken in ourselves and in the world. The Spirit and the creation itself groan over the world's chaos. As we join in, our groans make it a three-part harmony.[7]

If he weeps over abused and abandoned children, starving Yemenis, and the millions of trafficking victims around the globe, how can we not let our tears join his in grief? To fail in the recovery of the art of lament is to fate ourselves to a diminished capacity for Christlike compassion.

Just ranting over the evil of the world and rushing headlong into the penalty phase may make us feel righteously superior, but it actually exposes our spiritual immaturity. No amount of brainy people working together, no politician or party, and no innovation of science can hold back the tide of our sin against one another. We weep with God as an admission that we have no quick fixes for our loveless world, as a confession that we trust him to do what we cannot, and as a declaration of our availability to partner with him.

---

4. John 11:35.
5. Eph 4:30.
6. Gen 6:6.

7. Rom 8:22–26. If creation mourns, how much more we who inhabit it in anticipation of the renewal of all things.

Richard Rohr says, "Saint Ephraim goes so far as to say until you have cried you don't know God."[8] Jesus is a "Man of sorrows, acquainted with grief."[9] If we want to be better acquainted with him we have to be acquainted with what grieves him most. Intimacy with God is more that memorizing theological factoids. It involves tuning into what makes him weep, and then weeping by his side.

Our connection with God deepens to the degree that we join him in the "fellowship of his sufferings,"[10] which positions us to receive redemptive remedies for other weepers. While our lament may or may not result in silver bullet solutions to a world dilapidated by sin and Satan, it will undoubtedly lead to kingdom-advancing responses on our part.

We don't mourn in hopeless capitulation. Our weeping is a precursor to redemptive actions to follow. We grieve the deplorable state of our world and then stand up to do what we can to change it. We see the change that needs to be made and become the change we want to see.

Ours is a hope-filled weeping into which our God invites us.[11]

> May God bless you with tears to shed for those who suffer pain, rejection, hunger and war, so that you may reach out your hand to comfort them and turn their pain to joy. (A Franciscan Benediction)

---

8. Rohr, *Jesus' Plan for a New World*, 113.

9. Isa 53:3.

10. Phil 3:10.

11. For more on the art of lament see these resources: Wiget, "Sometimes You Just Gotta"; Wiget, "Recovering the Christian Art"; Wiget, "'Man of Sorrows."

Meekness: The Ego at Rest

Blessed are the meek for they will inherit the earth.
—MATT 5:5

This does not mean "blessed are they who are endowed with a tranquil natural temperament, who are not easily moved to anger, who are always quiet and obedient, who do not naturally resist." Still less does it mean "blessed are they who passively submit to unjust oppression."
—THOMAS MERTON[1]

IF IT'S TRUE, AS I've suggested, that Jesus implied a sequence of attitudes here, wherein one opens the way to the next, wouldn't it stand to reason that the *poor in spirit* would *mourn* their poverty and that a "meek" spirit would logically follow? If we possess honest-to-God grief over how spiritually impoverished we humans are, meekness is almost sure to come next.

Jesus seeks to destabilize our arrogance and construct a new way of thinking and acting in its place. The blessedness of the meek is another great example of a kingdom quality wherein *up is down* and *down is up*, especially when you consider the promise attached to it that the meek are granted the earth as their inheritance.

Remember that for the "middle-class in spirit" life is *their* film and the planet is *their* stage. They get top billing and the rest of us are just playing bit parts in support of their stardom. They might allow Jesus to play some part in their story, but they get the credit and everyone, including him, has

---

1. Merton, *Nonviolent Alternative*, 92.

to read off the script written for them. They seem to intend to "inherit the earth" without any assistance from above.

Though baited by Saul to attempt to win the kingdom in a duel, David learned that meekness works better[2] and saves us from unnecessary injury and wasted adrenaline. "My sacrifice, O God is a broken spirit," he confessed. "A broken and contrite heart you, God, will not despise."[3] In another place the Psalmist sang of how he calmed himself with the notion that he was like a "weaned child with its mother; like a weaned child I am content."[4]

The ego of the meek is an ego at rest. It's not haughty or hungry for praise. It's not restless or demanding like a baby still on the breast, nor does it clamor to be spoon-fed with "atta-boys." It's content.

America's worship of success is toxic to meekness. Pride feeds on status, power, and wealth, which is why it's so hard for the rich person to enter the kingdom. Regrettably, the Western Church is no less obsessed with climbing the ladder whose top wrung is obscured in the clouds. A cursory look at church history might lead one to conclude that *blessed are the politically powerful, successful, and the well-connected.*

"Humility," said Mother Teresa, "is nothing but the truth," the truth about who we are and what we are.[5] The meek recognize that truth and have no need to vaunt themselves. The truly meek are amazed that God and others think so well of them.

Humility is when *I* admit my spiritual poverty to you. Meekness is "Humility 2.0." It's when I'm willing for *you* to point out my poverty to me. Someone said, "If you realize that you are not wise, do not be angry if someone else should agree! You would be a hypocrite to think lowly of yourself but then expect others to think highly of you."

The meek are not defensive. They make no excuses for their failures. While they fight for the rights of others, they leave their own rights in God's hands. If you're thinking that taking Jesus' scandalous Sermon seriously will make you look weak, you might well be right, but if you're meek you won't care!

---

2. Ps 37:11.
3. Ps 51:17.
4. Ps 131:1–2.
5. Poplin, *Finding Calcutta*, 64.

Part Two | Utterly Upside-Down Attitudes

In this section we will explore the nature of the meek spirit, identify its central place in the Sermon, how it behaves as a witness in the public square, and in its radical response to enemies.

> Lord, we pray you will keep us humble enough to learn from those whom we least expect to be our teachers. Help us to listen for your truth, even in the words of our enemies.[6]

---

6. Claiborne, *Common Prayer*, 105.

Secure Enough to Serve

As we pick up the tools of servanthood (towel and basin) and wash each other's feet, the distinction between master and servant fades. We become servants to one another in God's flat kingdom.

—Donald Kraybill[1]

THE MEEK BRIDLE THEIR lust for power and live to serve others. "The 'politics' of the Kingdom," says Scott Bessenecker, "has more to do with meekness, submission and dying to self than it does with exercising authority to increase *my share* in this life."[2]

Some outside observers evaluate Jesus' words about being good to our enemies and forgiving trespassers as weakness, even masochistic. Yet the meek aren't necessarily shy, the mild-mannered, or the unassertive. They're the self-controlled who don't shrink back but willingly choose to yield. It's not that they are too scared to do otherwise, but voluntarily surrender the kind of power that could otherwise be used to get their way by any means necessary.

There's an old saying, "Anyone who thinks it's weak to be meek should try being meek for a week!" (Say that out loud for full effect.) Ironically it takes a lot of strength to be meek. Not the kind of strength you get in the gym, but the kind you get on your knees—so to speak.

Meekness is not the default position of our broken humanity. Even regenerated humanity doesn't arrive at meekness involuntarily. You don't just wake up one morning, make a resolution, and succeed at it. You don't

---

1. Kraybill, *Upside-Down Kingdom*, 145.
2. Bessenecker, *How to Inherit the Earth*, 53. Emphasis mine.

Part Two | Utterly Upside-Down Attitudes

achieve a broken spirit so much as *receive* it in your own post-crucifixion resurrections. The harsh reality is that meekness requires dying. That's why so few of us pursue it.[3]

Who but Jesus could say with a straight face and without pretense, "I am meek and lowly in heart"?[4] Yet he never showed the slightest sign of cowardice. Instead of commissioning legions of angels at his disposal, he permitted a relatively meager cohort of soldiers to take him and nail him to a cross. That's meekness—power under the control of the powerful.

Though he had alternative forms of transportation available to him, on his coronation day Jesus rode *meekly*[5] into Jerusalem on a donkey. He could've ordered his men: "Bring me a white stallion of regal stature with a gold-plated saddle." But he's a different kind of monarch, the kind who rides into town on the steed of a poor man. He could've been bullish and backed it up, but chose instead to be "harmless as a dove."

What but meekness could motivate the Lord of the universe to wash his friends' dusty feet? Instead of royal symbols like sword and chariot he made use of a servant's basin and towel, showing them he was secure enough to serve. He *knew* what he had, where he came from, and where he was going, and *therefore* played the servant.[6] Instead of using all the power of heaven at his disposal to subjugate potential followers by force, he bent low and did what lowly servants do.

But class wasn't dismissed until he commanded them (and us): "You also should wash one another's feet." The basin and towel are not his exclusive possessions. He bequeathed the tools of the servant's trade to us and called us to divest ourselves of our distinguishing vestments in order to wash feet. Herein is the essence of meekness.

It's not that the meek lack self-respect, for theirs is rooted in something other than possessions, prowess, or power. They revel in their value to God who paid such an exorbitant price for them. They have been "set free from the stifling atmosphere of pleasing others and fitting into the little patterns that they dictate."[7]

It should be noted that we don't get a vote in the kind of feet we're willing to wash. Our Prototype cleaned the feet of those who, with barely

---

3. Bessenecker, *How to Inherit the Earth*, 54.
4. Matt 11:29.
5. Matt 21:5.
6. John 13:3.
7. Gal 6:14, The Message.

latched sandals, finished drying the dishes, and fled the scene only to deny even knowing him! Not to mention the one who left the meal halfway through, running on his newly washed feet to sell out the Master for a slave's price. He lifted up his clean "heel"[8] and kicked Jesus in the heart.

The preposterous practice of footwashing is complicated by the distinct possibility that we too will be called upon to serve *foe* as well as *friend*. He washed the feet of deserters, deniers, and betrayers, after which he bequeathed towel and basin to them—to us!

---

8. Ps 41:9.

Half-Blind Eye Surgeons

Do not judge, or you too will be judged. For in the same way you judge others, you will be judged, and with the measure you use, it will be measured to you.

—Matt 7:1–2

I have never met a man I could despair of after discerning what lies in me apart from the grace of God.

—Oswald Chambers[1]

For two chapters (eighty-two verses, but who's counting?) Jesus had been raising the bar more and more on the ethics that reflect his upside-down social order. He knew how ready we are to apply his standards to everyone but ourselves, so he warned us against judging.

> What about those people?
> They don't love their enemies!
> They don't keep her oaths!
> They're all a bunch of Mammon-loving posers!

Instead of asking God to remove our flaws, we turn our attention to the flaws of others. It's a favorite anti-kingdom tactic to expect others to do what we're not willing to do. We may like playing the part of the Holy Spirit but there's only one of him. And it's not you—or me.

So, don't judge people. Not everyone's as good as you—or me!

---

1. Chambers, *My Utmost for His Highest*, 201.

The meek don't succumb to such self-righteousness. Their own planks come into view before others' splinters. They take into account that their vision probably isn't exactly twenty-twenty.

The un-meek tend to try to make themselves larger by making others smaller. When we say, "How bad he is!" what we really mean is, "How good I am!" Someone said, "It's impossible to love someone you disagree with when you secretly believe they need Jesus more than you do!" But the *ego at rest* has no need to put others down, even if they are Republicans or Democrats, Baptists or Pentecostals, billionaires or beggars.

Righteousness is fetching. Self-righteousness, not so much. Some people's passion for righteousness makes them rigid. Righteousness unmodified by meekness is unattractive and Pharisaical. "Search for this person's defects in your own heart," says Anthony De Mello, "and your annoyance will turn to gratitude that his or her behavior has led you to self–discovery."[2]

Unrighteous judging has a lot to do with assuming knowledge of another person's motives. We assume we know what's behind someone else's behavior, but we can't know more than can be known about the contents of another's heart. This is not to say that we are incapable of righteously drawing certain conclusions about a person based on the circumstantial evidence of their behavior. But we would be advised not to do so on impulse or based on prejudice. The meek proceed with caution.

Who in their right mind would want God to judge them as they've unjustly judged others? Fortunately, God judges us through the lens of Jesus' sacrifice, which should give us a not-so-subtle clue as to how we might consider judging others!

Planks, Splinters, and Eye Surgery

> Why do you look at the speck of sawdust in your brother's eye and pay no attention to the plank in your own eye? How can you say to your brother, 'Let me take the speck out of your eye,' when all the time there is a plank in your own eye? You hypocrite, first take the plank out of your own eye, and then you will see clearly to remove the speck from your brother's eye. (Matt 7:3–5)

---

2. As quoted in Moore, *Following the Call*, 282.

There's only one thing worse than the blind leading the blind, and that's a blind eye surgeon! Eye surgery is a delicate proposition and requires full use of one's faculties. It's not reassuring when the surgeon half blindly stumbles in your direction with scalpel in hand!

Meek people are aware of their own view-obscuring planks and they cooperate with the Spirit in their removal. They're self-aware rather than self-righteous. They're neither arrogant nor ignorant of the flaws of others. In fact, love motivates the meek soul to deal with their own planks *so they can see better* to assist their brothers and sisters to remove their splinters. The lesson here is not "Live and let live," but "Work on yourself so as to facilitate the work of the Spirit in others."

Leaving a painful foreign object in someone's eye is not really the most loving thing to do. The meek person *reaches out* as a servant rather than *reaching down* like a judge would from their bench to sentence a criminal.

"Don't Judge!"

I've heard people say, "The Bible says, you're not supposed to judge," when what they seem to really mean is "You're not supposed to judge *me*!" They don't care if you judge someone else; in fact, they're usually happy to help.

It is not judging per se, but *self-righteous* judging that the meek avoid. There's a difference between *making a moral judgment* and *being judgmental*. After all, just a breath or two later Jesus warns us to discern the disparity between a sheep in his own skin and a sheepskin with a wolf in it![3] He goes on to say that there's a qualitative difference between a true prophet and a false one, between a sheep and a goat, and between a mere *believer* and a true *behaver*. We need to be able to discern the difference.

On another occasion he warned, "Stop judging by mere appearances and make a right judgment."[4] Pronouncing judgment on someone is not "right judgment." Distinguishing right from wrong and *damning* those who do wrong are not the same thing. To *correct* is one thing, to *condemn*, another.

---

3. Matt 7:15.
4. John 7:24.

Judging versus Prophetic Critique

> Is it our place to make moral judgments about the current upon which our culture floats?
>
> Is it proper to challenge the anti-kingdom with upside-down kingdom values?
>
> Is it legitimate, even called for, when done in the right spirit and with our own logs in our eyes shaved down to a minimum, to speak truth to power?

If the church, as Martin Luther King claimed, is the *conscience of the state* then we cannot permit our culture to tumble over the falls without a warning. If we fail to recapture our prophetic voice we will forfeit our moral authority and doom the church to triviality.

The meek don't expect pre-Christians to act like Christians. They don't club people over the head with Bible verses about hell and damnation while parading down Main Street with pictures of aborted babies. But they do disrupt the dysfunction of the social order, point their communities toward *a more perfect union*, and hold their leaders accountable to the task of working for *liberty and justice for all*. And they do it with "gentleness and respect."[5]

Don't Feed the Animals!

In the next breath, Jesus changes the metaphor from eye surgery to feeding farm animals. "Do not give dogs what is sacred; do not throw your pearls to pigs. If you do, they may trample them under their feet, and turn and tear you to pieces" (Matt 7:6).

In other words, *don't force feed people the truth. It may be precious to you but if they're not ready for it yet, don't be in a hurry to deal with the splinter in their eye. They might jump off the table and turn the scalpel on you. For your sake and theirs, be patient and use a little discretion.*

We might remind ourselves of this when on impulse we toss meme grenades into social media "conversations" on politics—as though it actually fosters people's pursuit of truth. Screaming into the digital ether, rather than cooling the temperature, inflames interactions beyond the point of producing even the faintest possibility of progress.

5. 1 Pet 3:15.

Part Two | Utterly Upside-Down Attitudes

The meek are patient. They constantly work on their own stuff, and when the time and place are right, they offer to help rather than cause harm to others.

The Meek and Name-Calling

Carelessly call a brother "idiot!" and you just might find yourself hauled into court. Thoughtlessly yell "stupid!" at a sister and you are on the brink of hellfire. The simple moral fact is that words kill.

—MATT 5:22, THE MESSAGE BIBLE

YOU'RE NOTHING TO ME! *You are worthless and beneath my consideration!* This is the message we convey when we call one another derogatory names. The contempt contained in labeling others seeks to diminish their inherent value. It views them as subhuman, unworthy of respect or dignity. "Contempt is inherently poisonous . . . it is withering to the human soul."[1]

Branding people like cattle, grouping them in insulting categories is one of our more popular pastimes and most effective ways of unraveling our social fabric. Labels are often libels and unworthy of the meek follower of Jesus.

We label people because it's easier than actually *understanding* them. The most efficient way to sling mud is to do it with a broad brush. Or would that be a broad shovel? Whichever it is, you get more mud slung in less time that way. It saves a lot of mental energy to just call someone a name or file them in a folder. It's easier to caricature people than to take the time to become acquainted with them as unique beloveds of God. The meek refuse to vilify others by pigeonholing them.

The reason labels are bad is they're too small to explain any image-bearing human. Each of us is bigger than any one label can contain. Keeping others small makes the labeler feel large.

1. Willard, *Divine Conspiracy*, 171.

Part Two | Utterly Upside-Down Attitudes

Life is too nuanced for any human to fit tidily into a prefab, hard-and-fast classification. Labelers love reducing others as one of *these* or one of *those*, one of *us* or one of *them*. Unlike the meek, they set people up as strawmen (or women) and incinerate them at will.

Anyone who believes that marriage should only be between a man and woman is automatically branded "homophobic." A person against abortion is anti-feminist and chauvinistic. Environmentalists are all "tree-hugging hippies!" (a friend of mine actually said this). And those who fight systemic injustice on behalf of the poor are deemed "socialists." These assumptions may or may not be true in some cases, but individuals must be judged on a case-by-case basis rather than painted with the broad brush of prejudice.

This sort of libelous labeling isn't how the meek roll. They don't "think of themselves more highly than they ought"[2] but "value others above themselves."[3] When they can't find a reason to speak well of someone, the meek will venture below their exterior and look for even the tiniest evidence of the *Imago Dei*.

---

2. Rom 12:3.
3. Phil 2:3.

The Costly Love of the Meek

I tell you, love your enemies and pray for those who persecute you, that you may be children of your Father in heaven. He causes his sun to rise on the evil and the good, and sends rain on the righteous and the unrighteous. If you love those who love you, what reward will you get?

—Matt 5:44–46

Love your enemy. It may be hazardous, but you must do it.

—Howard Thurman[1]

Strap on your seatbelt for this is where the Sermon gets perilous. If Jesus demands anything that is more contrary to the culture of the commonplace than this, I don't know what it is. So, before continuing you might want to take a deep cleansing breath or two and ask the Spirit to speak to you about the people you don't like. And while you're at it, you might also include those who don't like *you* very much.

The default response for many readers of this portion of the address is to spend a lot of effort crafting exemptions to the rule of this kind of costly love. If I could, I'd invent a loophole to get me off the hook of loving my enemies, believe me I would—maybe something along the lines of pleading insanity. If nothing else, I could hide behind the popular alibi that only spiritual superheroes like Mother Teresa and Bishop Tutu could do it.

---

1. Thurman, *Jesus and the Disinherited*, 100.

Part Two | Utterly Upside-Down Attitudes

When all else fails, I'm left with facing my failings, pinning down my flesh for a count of ten (eleven just to be sure), and devoting myself to living beyond human means.

These enemy-love ethics can only be cultivated by internalizing the attitudes Jesus calls "blessed," especially this one on *meekness*. Only truly inwardly governed meek people can live into this kind of goodness—the kind that surpasses Pharisaical goodness. It's the meek that are most apt to express unconditional love to people *above* them, *below* them, and *against* them.

Those *above us* exploit the power differential between us for their benefit and slap us around (on the "right cheek") from their social, racial, or economic class atop our own. There are others *below us*, people over whom we have some sort of privilege or power. And, of course, there will always be people who are *against us* whose path runs in the opposite direction as ours and deliberately run into us on their way. The meek find it in their hearts to love even the most challenging image-bearing people.

The enemy-love message is not exactly what you'd call "attractional." Sadly, it's easier to gather a crowd with the message about a God who blesses our battles and hates our enemies as much as we do. Fear, anger, and hate are more popular than love and more natural to our darker selves. Unrestricted love is neither popular nor natural. It might fit nicely on a billboard or in a country song, but when it comes to actually practicing the kind of love Jesus commands, we'd much rather love in the abstract. "The first step toward love is a common sharing of a sense of mutual worth and value," wrote Howard Thurman. "This cannot be discovered in a vacuum or in a series of artificial or hypothetical relationships. It has to be in a real situation, natural, free."[2]

Loving our enemies is not for the sake of superior piety or because it's a winning strategy to get them to love us back. (Nelson Mandela said he'd never met an enemy that he didn't try to turn into a friend!) We're to love our enemies because *God* loves them. It's his nature to love, and he does it indiscriminately. In our quest to be like him we have to aspire to love like he does.

Loving our "own kind" and those who already love us is *easy love*. Where's the *surpassing righteousness* or reward in that? It brings God maximum glory when we love unconditionally and comprehensively. The litmus test for whether or not we love God is how we love our neighbor.

---

2. Thurman, *Jesus and the Disinherited*, 98.

The Costly Love of the Meek

And the most stringent test for whether we love our neighbor is how we love our enemies who, by the way, are also our neighbors. "There is a subtle pride in holding onto our hatreds as justified," says Walter Wink, "as if our enemies had passed beyond even God's capacity to love and forgive."

Jesus wasn't proposing an ethical system to adhere to, but invites us into a life of love that transcends formulas. Genuine love pushes us beyond duty. If the ethical question is, "What is required?" then love says, I will do *more*. Jesus calls us beyond the law in order to fulfill it.

Love Without Limits

If you love only those who love you, what reward is there for that? Even corrupt tax collectors do that much.
—Matt 5:46, NLT

To love the Roman meant first to lift him out of the general classification of enemy. The Roman had to emerge as a person.
—Howard Thurman[1]

Who loves a tax collector? Pretty much only other tax collectors, I suppose!

Instead of imitating God's indiscriminate love, we tend to love with predetermined limits and therefore copy cultural norms instead of the norms of the kingdom.

Limited-love people limit their love to people who love them. They draw a boundary around their own kind, a border that typically contains people of similar race, class, or culture. The line drawn around their love spawns a spirit of superiority over those outside the line.

The white landlord who rents only to people born with his same hue breaks God's heart, not to mention a few laws. Why? Because those otherwise hued are the "neighbors" Jesus told us to love. The landlord might not want them as neighbors, but what he doesn't realize is that, by token of our universally shared humanity, they already are!

---

1. Thurman, *Jesus and the Disinherited*, 113.

Casting a hated, half-breed Samaritan as the hero in the story who comes to the aid of a Jew in Jesus' day would be equivalent to a gay black guy in rural Arkansas rescuing a dying white supremacist, nursing him back to health, and paying all his medical bills!

Jesus knew that his fellow Jews loved their own kind over all non-Jews, and had biblical verses as well as religious traditions to support their prejudices. Mostly they hated their occupying Roman oppressors. Some might say for good reason. Reasons notwithstanding, he refused to let his brethren off the hook even if the soldiers treated them like slaves—slapping them around, suing them for their pennies, and forcing them to carry their loads. It's one thing to succumb to oppression and another to love your oppressors. Jesus demands the latter—a love without limits.

One church in India placed a sign on the wall as you enter their worship facility: "Leave behind all race and class distinction as you enter here." Loving exclusively those in our own ethnic, socioeconomic, or national distinctive paves the path to the land of ugly "isms," such as nepotism, racism, and nationalism.

"Isms" easily become idols. Hard hearts and hostility toward people of other cultures and colors is an idolatrous worship of nationalistic identity that the meek believer knows nothing of. Allegiance to God is the lens through which the meek view all others.

"For white evangelicals to embrace a platform and advocacy that promotes, prioritizes, and defends America above all and over all is to embrace an idolatry that has only ever proven disastrous," says Fuller Seminary President Dr. Mark Labberton. "A legitimate debate about immigration laws and practices is surely necessary, as difficult as it may be. But that debate is distorted if it begins with nationalistic assumptions."[2]

It's easier to caricature the "others" when they're a mere digital abstraction on the internet. Actual empathy, on the other hand, is bred by proximity. We can't very well empathize with the plight of those outside our group, ethnicity, or class without some form of proximity to them. (Facebook "friendships" and Twitter followers don't count.)

---

2. Labberton, "Political Dealing," para. 26. Labberton went on to say in that same talk to evangelical leaders on April 16, 2018: "When it seems that white evangelicals endorse self-interest through political speech that is nationalistic and demeaning to others, our central commitments do not reflect Jesus Christ, but rather a cold, white heart" (para. 27).

PART TWO | UTTERLY UPSIDE-DOWN ATTITUDES

Exceptions or the Rule?

Before delving more deeply into the details of Jesus' third way, let's get something out of the way. I can hardly remember having a discussion on his enemy-love teaching, replete with other cheek turning, extra mile going, and overcoat donating, where someone doesn't propose a litany of exceptions.

> *What do I do after I turn the other cheek and he slugs me on that cheek too?*
>
> *Does Jesus expect me to be a doormat when my boss harasses me?*
>
> *What if someone breaks into my house and threatens my family?*
>
> *Should a woman stay and take it from her abusive husband?*
>
> *This just doesn't work today!*

It's not good exegesis if and when the exceptions to the rule (even legitimate ones) become *the rule itself*. Exceptions too easily become *excuses* for not following the rule. Some have created warehouses full of exceptions into which almost any excuse can be tossed and stored for ready access. Inevitably then, Jesus' third way morphs into an exceptional brand of Christianity instead of the way *all* Christians must conduct themselves at *all* times. When his actual radical standards get buried under an avalanche of caveats it becomes unattainable for the rank-and-file believer to emerge out from under it and live God's way.

> "Turning the other cheek" is not intended to be a legal requirement to be applied woodenly in every situation but as an impetus for discovering creative alternatives that transcend the only two that we are conditioned to perceive; fight or flight.[3]

If cheek-turning is not rooted in love, it may do more harm than good to the bully and to the bullied. Using this as a "technique," apart from the incentive of genuine *agape*, may increase the contempt of the bully and the insecurity of the bullied. Love is the key.

Don't forget, the Blessed Attitudes are the base of everything, which inevitably lead to blessed actions. Everything he teaches throughout the body of the Sermon is like a fruit tree that grows out of the soil of meekness, mercy, peacemaking, and so on. Therefore, dig down deep and plant

---

3. Wink, *Jesus and Nonviolence*, 44.

the seeds of love in the fertile soil of meekness, water them regularly, pull the weeds often, give them plenty of sun, and watch the tree grow and bear otherwise unattainable fruit.

As we'll see, turning the other cheek and going the extra mile, rather than producing doormats, is intended to restore dignity to the victim and put an end to the cycle of humiliation.

More or Less Like Jesus

Either we find the God who causes his sun to rise on the evil as well as the good or we may have no more sunrises.
—Walter Wink[1]

He taught us a new social order and then bequeathed it to our care to model and teach others. Even those still living outside his benevolent rule can benefit from a world in which his kingdom is approximated.

We sing in our worship songs and claim in our confessions that we want to be like Jesus. I suspect our aspirations, though sincere, exist mostly in the abstract, especially as we think of loving people who don't return the favor. Remember, this is the One who, when breathing his last, forgave his torturers! His subversive methods were anything but weak and nothing if not meek.

He vetoes violence as a means of setting things right and advancing his Kingdom. As they "spit in his face, struck him with their fists, and slapped him"[2] he practiced what he preached and loved them nonetheless.

Given that Peter did his *Lancelot* imitation in the garden and sliced off a guy's ear in defense of the Lord, it's possible that he missed the lecture on enemy love just months before. The issue is not whether to resist or not, for neither flight nor fight (passive submission or violent retaliation) are the Jesus way. So he stooped down, retrieved the severed ear, and grafted it back in place. In so doing, he demonstrated to everyone there that his

---

1. Wink, *Jesus and Nonviolence*, 34.
2. Matt 26:67.

MO is not one of helplessness, but rather of generous compassion. His love contains within it a redemptive power.

Sadly, many American Christians seem to relate more to Ayn Rand's unmistakably anti-kingdom ideology of "Objectivism" than to the utterly opposite teaching and example of Jesus. She proposed that we're all an end to ourselves and must live for our own sakes and self-interest. The highest moral purpose of humans, to her way of thinking, is to pursue our own happiness in spite of how it might impact others. She objected to Jesus' cross as an example of sacrificing ourselves for our "inferiors."

Her philosophy reminds me of the mob that preferred Barabbas and his violent revolutionary approach to Roman oppression. Jesus rules from a cross and makes peace through sacrifice. They mistook his meekness for weakness and failed to appreciate his choice to express his omnipotence through love.

Some think he must've been speaking hypothetically when he told us to love our enemies and turn the other cheek. After all, didn't he make a whip and turn over tables in the temple? Sounds pretty harsh for a guy who preaches meekness.

First of all, his was not some sort of temper tantrum, but a prophetic action highlighting the injustice of the powerful profiting from the weak. It doesn't say he *used* the whip, only that he made it. And if he did use it, I doubt that he used it on people, even though they were deserving. If he swung it at all it was to shoo out the animals being sold for profit.

We learn from him that meekness isn't for weaklings compliantly cowering in the corner. For a Man with more than twelve legions of angels at his command, in his zeal for his Father's house he could well have done unforgettable destruction that day but restrained himself to chipping a few tables and shaking up some goats. He modeled the sort of self-control commensurate with a true spirit of meekness.

Who's to say that he wasn't tempted on that day to put a real beat down on those who were beating down the people he loved? If Jesus was "tempted in every way we are"[3] I can only assume that he thought about using his strength to blast his enemies rather than bless them. Thankfully he refrained.

Can't you just see him as a youth, rather than opening a crater on the schoolyard and throwing the class bully into it, he taps into the Spirit's strength and resists? Which is not to say that he stood passively by and did

---

3. Heb 4:15.

nothing. In fact, I can see him standing in-between the bully and his prey, and absorbing the blows in his own body. Instead of harming the harmer he absorbs the harm and sets the victim free.[4]

It's not as though he was any less opposed to Roman occupation than were the resistance fighters of his day, the trained assassins who were known, for good reason, as "daggermen" or Zealots. But he consistently practiced an entirely different way of treating enemies, and if we want to be like him, we must follow his lead.

The mantra in most secular, not to mention way too many *spiritual* circles, boils down to "Might is Right." They think in terms of conquest and power, whereas Jesus' kingdom runs on an entirely different fuel called *meekness*. And he commissions us, not as aggressors, but as vulnerable "lambs among wolves."

Wait! Who "Inherits the Earth"?

What's this about the meek *inheriting the earth*? One comedian quipped that it's because they'll be too timid to refuse it! Not exactly. It's more likely that the meek conduct themselves as though they possess *nothing* and are therefore the most likely candidates to inherit *everything*. They don't conquer or take over the earth. Instead, they "inherit" it from their Father who knows that these are the kind of people he can trust with his planet.

> The reason that the meek will inherit the earth is that they are naturally disposed to use power in the way it was designed by God to be used—as a guard for the weak and to preserve the common good. A life lived in simplicity, humility and obscurity will be a very handy asset at the end of the game when God is looking for meek people to put in charge.[5]

Sad to say, it's not just the anti-kingdom culture that prefers swords to plowshares. An immense swath of the Western Church prides herself on power, wealth, and political influence. She rejects the footwashing basin for bravado and the towel for pomposity! She may not be going on actual crusades to conquer the heathen in the Holy Land, but this antithesis of the spirit of meekness is alive and well in many Christian circles today.

---

4. Rom 15:3.
5. Bessenecker, *How to Inherit the Earth*, 24.

The meek lobby for the lowest seats and are therefore often placed in the highest ones. Their love for the most unlovable qualifies them. They're more concerned with justice for the most vulnerable than they are with their own status. "The future of the world will be in the hands of those who serve and save the world."[6]

---

6. Jones, *Unshakable Kingdom*, 197.

Meek Enough To Love Those Who Don't Love Us Back

You have heard that it was said, "Eye for eye, and tooth for tooth." But I tell you, do not resist an evil person. If anyone slaps you on the right cheek, turn to them the other cheek also. And if anyone wants to sue you and take your shirt, hand over your coat as well. If anyone forces you to go one mile, go with them two miles. Give to the one who asks you, and do not turn away from the one who wants to borrow from you.
—Matt 5:38–42

Returning violence for violence multiplies violence, adding deeper darkness to a night already devoid of stars.
—Martin Luther King Jr.

"If a man smite you on one cheek, smash him down; smite him hip and thigh, for self-preservation is the highest law. He who turns the other cheek is a cowardly dog—a Christian dog."[1]

As he was apt to do, in order to illuminate his third way of nonviolent resistance, Jesus uses a string of wise and witty images about *eyes, teeth, cheeks, shirts, coats,* and *mile markers.* Each of these captures the imagination and puts his teaching into shoe leather. We'll unpack some of these here and more of them in later chapters when we talk about mercy, peacemaking, and the Christian response to persecution.

---

1. From Arthur Desmond's book, *Might is Right.* It's no wonder that Anton LaVey dedicated his *Satanic Bible* to Desmond and other secular humanist teachers!

Your Eye for Mine

People treat their enemies in one of three ways: *demonically, legalistically,* or *christianly.* Returning evil for good is demonic. Giving back good for good and evil for evil (eye for an eye) is legalistic. Many Christians practice this second way without giving it a second thought. Someone puts out your eye and you put out his! In that case, their conduct determines yours and you're just an echo of them. Christian practitioners live by a different code altogether, a righteousness that "surpasses"[2] all others, a third way that reciprocates good for evil.

Our social media debates about religion and politics these days are rife with eye-for-an-eye justice, or worse, my one eye for both of yours! And consider yourself lucky that I don't consider breaking your nose (that is, your digital nose)! If you knock out one of my teeth, I can knock out all of yours and my Facebook "friends" will applaud me for it!

The law of the jungle is: For every action, there's an *unequal* opposite overreaction. But Jesus, who fulfilled the spirit of the law, proposes a better way, the way of love. And if his way is not workable, "then the heart of the Sermon does not beat—it is a carcass, a dead body of doctrine."[3]

The Bully's Backhand

> If anyone slaps you on the right cheek, turn to them the other cheek also. (Matt 5:39)

As was his custom, in framing his non-violent resistance ethic, Jesus piques our imagination with parables and hyperbole. His graphic examples point us in the direction of his inverted-kingdom response to bullying and injustice.

The question is how on earth do we apply what he's saying? I mean when was the last time you were slapped in the face? Never, I hope! But if you have been, no doubt you'll recall the humiliation of it, especially if it was a *backhanded* slap. That's the kind that Jesus describes here.

In the East, to backhand someone is the grossest form of insult. Think of it as someone spitting in your face. Epictetus, who was born a slave and later became a Greek Stoic philosopher, said a slave would rather be

---

2. Matt 5:20.
3. Jones, *Unshakable Kingdom*, 150.

PART TWO | UTTERLY UPSIDE-DOWN ATTITUDES

beat to death than slapped in the face. In order to put them in their place, higher-ups backhand their "inferiors." An abusive husband backhands his wife to show her who is boss. It's a bitter reminder of his power over her powerlessness.

There's no doubt that Jesus had often observed Romans backhanding his Jewish brethren to reinforce their upper hand. And from his own personal experience he knew the feeling that the slapper intends to convey (Matt 26:67). If Jesus had struck back, I wouldn't be writing this and you wouldn't be reading it. It would've made him too much like us and therefore unable to save us from ourselves.

> When they hurled their insults at him, he did not retaliate; when he suffered, he made no threats. Instead, he entrusted himself to him who judges justly.[4]

Who could be more qualified to command us to respond in like manner?

Let's get this cheek-turning thing straight. Slapping someone on the "right cheek" requires using your right hand in a backhanded action. The alternative would be an open left hand, which is unlikely for any right-handed slapper. (Roleplay these two options with a friend and you'll see what I mean. But do it in slow motion and preferably with someone whom you have no desire to actually slap!)

What we're talking about here is an open-handed backhand slap and not to a closed fist punch in the face. You punch someone with a closed fist that you want to *harm*, whereas you backhand the one you intend to *humiliate*. Jesus is talking about *insults*, not *fistfights*. Self-defense doesn't seem to be the issue here, but rather to an underdog's response to an insulting action by a *bigger dog*.

Though a punch is meant to inflict physical harm, the slap is intended to shame the victim psychologically. It's a show of power and superiority over a weaker person. They convey the message, "Can't you see that you're insignificant and worth nothing to me?"[5] By turning the other cheek we let the bully know that we won't be so easily humiliated.

More on the "slap" later.

---

4. 1 Pet 2:23.

5. Both Jeremiah and Job spoke of the "disgrace" of this sort of slap (Lam 3:30; Job 16:10).

Wait. My Coat Too?

> If anyone wants to sue you and take your shirt, hand over your coat as well. (Matt 5:41)[6]

This is part of the same morally daring action as cheek-turning. The debtor, so poor he owns nothing with which to pay his debt except the clothes on his back, stands before his creditor with both shirt and coat in his hand. It's kind of a dare: *You have my shirt and coat but you can't take my soul or my self-respect!*

In this, and all of these deliberately graphic scenarios, the hope is that the oppressor will be conscience stricken and will, if not forgive the debt, at least learn to treat his debtor with respect. In each of these vignettes Jesus teaches us how to retain our self-respect by following his example. "They cannot take away our self-respect if we do not give it to them," said Gandhi.

Two Miles! Are You Kidding?

> If anyone forces you to go one mile, go with them two miles. (Matt 5:41)

Roman law entitled its soldiers to force any Jew into carrying his heavy military gear for a mile. Imagine how that made the Jews feel, being treated with all the respect of a pack mule. It was much more than the physical strain or the inconvenience of being conscripted while on their way to work. It was the humiliation of it all! Why then would Jesus tell them to go *two miles*?

"The teaching of the Sermon the Mount," says Oswald Chambers, "is not—Do your duty, but—Do what is not your duty."[7] Remember, the *surpassing righteousness* that befits true kingdom people is a theme throughout the Discourse. In this case it surpasses it by a "mile"! It would be all I could do to refrain from spitting on it (if not worse) before handing it back after the first mile. But Jesus invites us into a better way, albeit a much more challenging way for which we need divine impetus.

---

6. The law states that in order to pay his creditor back the debtor may have to pledge his cloak. In which case the creditor is to return it by nightfall so that the poor man won't freeze in the cold (Deut 24:10–13; Exod 22:25–27). The creditor is only entitled by law to take the debtor's shirt, but Jesus tells him to give him his coat also.

7. Chambers, *My Utmost for His Highest*, 219.

PART TWO | UTTERLY UPSIDE-DOWN ATTITUDES

This *extra mile* ethic is another example of a morally daring act of resisting an oppressor without emulating him, neutralizing his inhumanity without mirroring it. Resisting with such unquenchable good will, you are saying, *I'm not serving you because I fear your authority or even your ability to harm or kill me. I do it freely because I choose to. I do it to imitate Jesus' higher standard.*

You're under the soldier's control for the first leg. After that you're walking in the freedom of your own choice. While the first might be considered *passive resistance*, the voluntary mile, which requires the strength of a meek spirit, is the kingdom way of *active nonviolent resistance*.

There might be a serendipitous evangelistic benefit here. Instead of cussing your bully under your breath, the second mile might just give you the time to become better acquainted, not as opponents, but as fellow image bearers. Your character has been put to the test, and having passed with flying colors, you might actually have the opportunity to share the good news with him. Once you've demonstrated God's stubborn love, you've gained sufficient credibility to invite your oppressor to taste and see for himself the goodness that comes only from the Lord!

Let's be honest, the way of Jesus doesn't always deescalate violence or prevent our suffering. The final Beatitude is proof of that: "Blessed are the persecuted." But these daring "third way" creative alternatives to violent resistance, along with practicing indiscriminate love, have the potential of breaking the cycle of injustice and humiliation. Our motive is not utilitarian, but love for others and obedience to God.

The Third Way

The stamp of the saint is that he can waive his own rights and obey the Lord Jesus.

—Oswald Chambers[1]

I like a story where the good guys win and the bad guys lose. To me, it's more irritating than entertaining when the protagonist ends up on the bottom? That's what's so fascinating, if not frustrating about our hero from heaven. The way our king wins (on a cross) seems so—*unkingly*. Jesus didn't even put up a fight on his own behalf, at least not in any sort of way that we would identify as a such. It might be said that he won by "losing."

While it's too multilayered to address all the reasons he chose to win this way, let's just say one takeaway is the counterintuitive notion that we fight best when we don't fight back! Though we typically presume that a victim has two choices: Strike back or cower in humiliation, Jesus prescribes a *third way*.

Let's turn back to the scene of the slap. (You might bring your role-playing friend back for more if they're willing to endure another faux fight.) Gently backhand them with your right hand on their right cheek and take notice that their face naturally recoils to their left.

So, when Jesus says, "Turn the other cheek," he seems to be telling us to turn our face *back toward our attacker* and look him in the eye. Refuse to retaliate with violence, but don't let him take away your dignity either. "Do not cower and do not punch back. Make sure the person looks into your

---

1. Chambers, *My Utmost for His Highest*, 222.

eyes and sees your sacred humanity, and it will become increasingly harder for that person to hurt you."[2]

The Amplified Bible corroborates this: "turn the other cheek and maintain your dignity, your self-respect, your poise." He's not asking us to put up with insults or cruelty as much as to demonstrate a fearless yet peaceful insistence on equal dignity with an oppressor.

Mahatma Gandhi, of whom it is said that he read from the Sermon on the Mount twice a day for the last forty years of his life (and he didn't even profess to be a Christian!) said: "Do what you like, I will match my capacity to suffer against your capacity to inflict that suffering, and I will wear you down with goodwill." This is the essence of nonviolent noncooperation.

Repaying a slap for a slap says, *You think you shame me? Well, I'll shame you instead! You're not stronger than me. In fact, I'm stronger than you! You want to fight? Then let's fight and may the best man win!!!* That's the eye-for-an-eye way, not the Jesus way.

In spite of lopsided physical strength, social position, or economic status, we resist the contempt others try to foist upon us by asserting our confidence as their equal. When we return blow for blow, we stoop to the bully's level and jump into the sewage of hatred with them. Even if we win the fight, we walk away smelling worse than when we began!

When he says, "Do not resist an evil person" (Matt 5:39) he uses a military term that denotes a violent reprisal, as in the eye-for-an-eye way.[3] (Too bad the Crusaders in medieval times didn't know this. Or they did and simply disregarded it.) His is not a strategy of resignation but counsel on how to exercise moral strength even when we are overpowered. The essence of self-respect is to refuse to be defined by those with the upper hand.

Again, Gandhi famously observed, "An eye for an eye makes the whole world blind." When the church is vengeful and vitriolic, we blind ourselves and the world from seeing Jesus.

Once you've turned your cheek and you're face to face with your oppressors, the ball is in their court. They can either backhand you again or punch you in the face (both of which are real possibilities). Or in the best-case scenario, you have paralyzed them to amazement. They won't know

---

2. Claiborne and Law, *Jesus for President*, 251.

3. Sider, *Speak Your Peace*, 34. Ron Sider says, "In forty-four of seventy-one uses in the Greek Old Testament, the word refers to armed resistance in military encounters" and cites Josephus who uses the word fifteen of seventeen times to refer to "violent struggle."

where to go from there and could actually surrender to the love that they see before them!

Even if they do up the ante and punch you in the face, they've lost the advantage of moral authority. They may well be forced to see you as an equal, one who could have fought back if you chose to, but didn't. Bullies don't like being put in that situation. Their power over you lies in their ability to humiliate. Refuse to be humiliated and you've at least *dented*, if not *destroyed* that power.

Turning the other cheek says: *I'm not going to hit you back. But you should know that I am an image bearer too, over which you have no absolute power. I refuse to be defined by your assessment of me. I know who I am and, regardless of how you treat me, you can never take that from me!*

This is where self-respect, self-control, and meekness intersect. When you *respond* to another's contempt in the Jesus way rather than *react* in your own way, you demonstrate the strength of your convictions while choosing to keep that strength under control. That's the essence of meekness!

Stoic passivity can be a cloak for weakness or fear. Jesus summons us to the kind of active resistance rooted in love that reveals true courage and strength of character. Anyone can strike back. It doesn't require great moral strength to retaliate. Jesus' third way is not for the weak, but exclusively for the meek.

Your opponents may use their weapon of choice but if you're meek you won't let them choose yours for you. When we turn our cheek, we choose the weapon of love. "Of all weapons," says Howard Thurman, "love is the most deadly and devastating, and few there be who dare trust their fate in its hands."[4] If you refuse to let them decide your reaction it proves that you are determined *from within*. While they may try to break your self-confidence, your response may break open their hearts so the Spirit can seep through the cracks.

N. T. Wright says that God's way of changing the world is not by sending in tanks. Instead, he sends in the meek. As Pope Francis recently declared, "A culture of nonviolence is not an unattainable dream, but a path that has produced decisive results. The consistent practice of nonviolence has broken barriers, bound wounds, healed nations."

As Gandhi was beginning to promote his nonviolent noncooperation movement in India, his friend and missionary E. Stanley Jones was skeptical. Later Jones wrote:

---

4. Thurman, *Deep Is the Hunger*, 11.

> The method of nonviolent noncooperation shook me and it shook the mighty British Empire. My objections melted away when I saw it in action—hot-tempered men and women taking suffering, not giving it; submitting to their heads being cracked under blows . . . going to jail without protest, asking for the severest penalty . . . and as they were being led out of court to prison, saying to the British judge: "Father, forgive them for they know not what they are doing." Hindus saying that to the Christian. . . . When it was pure nonviolence uncontaminated by hate, it was power—pure power![5]

The repressive Marcos regime was toppled in the Philippines by unrelenting peaceful popular pressure. With its campaign of nonviolent resistance, the African National Congress brought down the brutal South African apartheid. Through boycotts, demonstrations, marches, and freedom rides, our own civil rights struggle in the United States dismantled much (yet not all) of our country's legalized white supremacy.

Mark Scandrette says, "Evil perpetuates evil until someone dares to break the cycle."[6] Instead of adding the fuel of revenge to the vicious cycle of hostility, Jesus posits creative alternatives to the typical anti-kingdom's revenge-driven tactics. Even in social media conversations a diplomatic approach tends to defuse the debate down to a more manageable temperature.

The value of returning verbal jab for jab quickly loses altitude like a skydiver whose chute won't open. On the other hand, "A gentle response defuses anger," says Solomon, "but a sharp tongue kindles a temper-fire."[7]

History, personal experience, and the Bible all say that revenge is a losing proposition, even if it appears to win temporarily. You might overpower your opponent's body but you haven't begun to touch his soul, which will most likely make him a worse enemy than before.

Jesus' *Third Way* is an act of obedience. If the kindness is returned in kind, great. But fidelity to Jesus' way trumps success. If we can't redeem our enemies at least we can retain our integrity. And at the end of the day that's a win.

You've won the battle over your own baser impulses by acting more like Jesus than you might have otherwise. Bow low and let that crown fall at his feet!

5. Jones, *Song of Ascents*, 97.
6. Scandrette, *Ninefold Path of Jesus*, 112.
7. Prov 15:1, The Message Bible.

The Meek Witness

You are the salt of the earth. But if the salt loses its saltiness, how can it be made salty again? It is no longer good for anything, except to be thrown out and trampled underfoot.

You are the light of the world. A town built on a hill cannot be hidden. Neither do people light a lamp and put it under a bowl. Instead they put it on its stand, and it gives light to everyone in the house. In the same way, let your light shine before others, that they may see your good deeds and glorify your Father in heaven.

—Matt 5:13–16

The Character of Our Influence Is the Influence of Our Character

On the heels of his list of blessed attitudes, Jesus describes our influence on the world as "salt and light." He inserts it there because the character of our influence is the influence of our character. Coaxing people into his upside-down kingdom is best done by "show and tell." If you don't show it, then please, for God's sake, don't tell it! It's only *good news* if it comes from a good person—not a perfect one, but one in which goodness undeniably presides and incrementally progresses.

The Bible is no survivalist manifesto. His address isn't just about how to withstand our unaccommodating world. Cowering in Christian ghettos bears no resemblance to the God-honoring faith of our fathers.

The acronym that Christians sometimes use to describe the purpose of the Bible, *Basic Instructions Before Leaving Earth*, reflects neither the Bible's true message nor the life and commission of Jesus. The implication is that we are just passing the time here while waiting for Jesus to return and whisk us away to heaven. He invites us to live a better way and partner with him to make a better world.

Our saltiness and light bearing are directly proportionate to how we live into these qualities of Christlike-ness. Without these we end up pushing people away from Christ rather than nudging them toward him. We bring heaven's kingdom to earth in proportion to the way we let heaven have its way in our way of living.

The world is decomposing. It needs salt. It's dark and needs light. As salt, we counter corruption and as light, we dispel darkness. (Yes, I did say "we," because he says *we are* salt and *we are* light.) If it sounds a bit daunting, it's because it is.

A Meek Witness Is Not a Weak Witness

As we've shown, meekness is anything but weakness. It's really the strongest form of strength, the kind of strength that's used for the benefit of others.

The meek witness that Jesus imagines doesn't cower behind church walls and rave against the wickedness of the outside world. A Christianity that is walled off from its host culture is one with a very short shelf life. The meek don't major in cursing the darkness but in shining the light that comes from the inside.

Let us not use the light to blind people, but to light things up so they can see Jesus. When our witness lacks meekness, we radiate more heat than light and scorch people instead of illuminating their path to God. "Pride makes us artificial; humility makes us real," says Thomas Merton. Ours is not a blistering evangelistic bluster, but one beggar telling another beggar where to find bread.

Mudslinging stump speech testimonies might give us a commanding appearance but won't win many people to Christ. Jesus sends us out as vulnerable and needy—*lambs among wolves*.[1] Meek and humble servants are best poised to attract people to the meek and humble Savior.

---

1. Luke 10:3.

Dim Lights and Unsalty Salt

> But if the salt loses its saltiness, how can it be made salty again? It is no longer good for anything, except to be thrown out and trampled underfoot. (Matt 5:13)

It's by being *different* that we make a difference and contribute to God's purpose of returning the world to its original rightside-upness. When our lives fail to reflect the character of Jesus our saltiness becomes absorbed by the world and provides no real benefit to those without Christ.

Technically, salt can't lose its saltiness. That is, sodium chloride is a very stable compound and can't be other than it is, though it can be washed away only to leave behind a white dust that may look like salt but isn't. At that point it's only good for filling potholes. If we lose our ability to promote and preserve what is good in the world, we mustn't be surprised when we are ignored, and like road dust, are "trampled underfoot." Losing our saltiness means we've lost our credibility and deserve to be ignored.[2]

In the same way, though it is the nature of light to shine, light can be clouded and lose the ability to illuminate. If we're just as greedy, self-indulgent, violent, and arrogant as the dominant culture, we become tasteless and useless—"no longer good for anything." Not exactly the legacy we were intended to leave!

City on a Hill

> A city on a hill cannot be hidden. (Matt 5:14)

Perched high above the valley below like a jewel in the daytime and a neon sign at night, Israel's capital city Jerusalem was on Jesus' mind as he compared it to our testimony in the world.

Ever since seventeenth-century Puritan John Winthrop urged his fellow pilgrims to live in such a way as to be a "city on a hill" in the New World, several US presidents on both sides of the aisle have used Jesus' phrase (most notably Ronald Reagan) as a metaphor for "American exceptionalism." Many have molded Jesus' words about the church's influence

---

2. The phrase "If the salt loses its saltiness" could be translated as "if the salt becomes foolish." See 1 Cor 1:20 and Rom 1:22 where the same Greek term is used.

in the world into their own preferred shape, claiming a privileged divine destiny for America as a nation among nations.

America is not, and never has been, God's instrument of salvation. To think otherwise is arrogant and parochial. "America—as are all nations—is a provisional structure sustained by God for maintaining security, order, and justice. America is important as an earthly kingdom, not as the kingdom of God."[3]

Our beloved country is indeed "exceptional" in many ways, though to claim its superiority to other nations, with a special relationship to God and a divinely appointed mission in the world, can't be proven without performing some mental jujitsu with the Bible and with history.

Americans are not God's chosen people, and America is not the New Israel or the "city on a hill." That distinction belongs exclusively to the body of Christ in *every nation*. We have a great country and our system of governance might well be the best in the world, but it's the church worldwide that emits divine light.

Every time in history the church has tried to sanitize a national identity and raise the Christian flag over a nation, a people group, or a political party, it has always turned out poorly! The late Billy Graham knew this when he said: "It would disturb me if there was a wedding between the religious fundamentalists and the political right. The hard right has no interest in religion except to manipulate it." Nonetheless the wedding *did* take place and the offspring that came of that union have not wielded the best influence on our culture.

This is not to say that the political left has any more right to wed the body of Christ. When it does, it does no less damage to both the state and the church. If we're to be the salt and light that Jesus imagined we must revel only in our marriage to our Heavenly Bridegroom and be faithful to him.

The "Social" Influence of Salt and Light

Walter Brueggemann says, "Don't tell Jesus that religion plays no part in the public arena or that faith is just a private matter between you and your Creator. He'll think you weren't listening."

In Jesus' day no civilization could survive without salt or light. Comparing us to both is the same as saying,

3. Benne, *Good and Bad Ways*, 203.

The Meek Witness

You are what the world needs in order to become everything it was created to be. Without you, humanity will never reach the height of God's dream for what it means to be truly human. You preserve the good and light the way forward!

Our responsibility to bring people into the kingdom through salvation is inextricably linked to our social responsibility to bring the ways of the kingdom down to earth. Our improved lives must improve the culture. Without doing our bit to make this a better place, we preach a nonsensical message of salvation with no visible evidence of an invisible God. We seek to "save souls" *and* partner with him to create a society that more closely reflects his kingdom. It's all part of God's saving act.

I love sharing Christ with pre-Christians. I even wrote a book on it called *Reaching Rahab: Joining God In His Quest For Friends*. That said, Jesus had a *holistic* world-changing project in mind when he commissioned us as "salt and light," a project that includes both personal evangelism and social change. Tim Keller writes, "To work against social injustice and to call people to repentance before God interlock theologically."[4] Racial reconciliation, a just distribution of power, a fair access to wealth and opportunity, and the abolition of human trafficking all go hand-in-hand with sharing the soul-saving message of Jesus.

For this reason, meek witnesses avoid toeing any party line in their efforts to improve the culture, but view their social responsibilities through a kingdom lens. God's new society requires the best in both conservative and liberal, Republican and Democrat influences. As Jim Wallis says, "The Right gets it wrong and the Left doesn't get it."[5] Our politics should be shaped through our faith, not the other way around.

The church has a mixed legacy when it comes to her socio-spiritual influence—some for good and some for bad. There were those, for instance, who propagated the transatlantic slave trade by twisting Scripture to justify their cruelty. Yet others pushed back against its evil by following their moral conscience influenced by an accurate interpretation of the very same book.

Born into slavery, Harriet Tubman was an American abolitionist who escaped her captors and subsequently made over a dozen missions to rescue enslaved people through her Underground Railroad. Tubman's Christian faith informed and inspired her courageous activism.

---

4. Keller, *Prodigal Prophet*, 94.
5. Wallis, *Christ in Crisis?*, 13.

Part Two | Utterly Upside-Down Attitudes

Rosa Parks respectfully declined when a bigoted Montgomery, Alabama bus driver ordered her to surrender her seat to a white person. Small in stature but large in faith, Parks was pulled off the bus and jailed. When she woke up that morning it hadn't occurred to her to incite a bus strike that would last 381 days. Nevertheless, her act of faith led to a Supreme Court decision that declared the laws that segregated buses in Alabama unconstitutional. Later she said, "God has always given me the strength to say what is right." These two very meek and very bold sisters were part of what Jesus meant when he said we are the "city on a hill."

According to Jesus, our radiance has more to do with *good works* than *good words*. It's what we *do in this world*, not just what we *say to this world* that lights the way to both personal salvation and social improvement.

Meek witnesses *demonstrate and declare* a kingdom that transforms hearts, homes, and whole cultures. As salt and light, together we have the ability to hinder, if not arrest the process of social decay. When we neglect the social implications of the gospel, our efforts to "win souls" disappear into abstractions. The meek live in such a way as to demand an *explanation* which leads to personal and social *renovation*.[6]

❊ ❊ ❊

As a bridge from meekness to the next Beatitude, "Blessed are those who hunger and thirst for righteousness," I commend to you a beautiful, yet dangerous prayer called, "The Litany of Humility." Here's a sample of it to whet your appetite:

> O Jesus! Meek and humble of heart, hear me.
> From the desire of being esteemed, deliver me, Jesus.
> From the desire of being extolled, deliver me, Jesus.
> From the desire of being honored, deliver me, Jesus.
> From the desire of being praised, deliver me, Jesus.
> From the desire of being preferred to others, deliver me, Jesus.
> From the desire of being consulted, deliver me, Jesus.
> From the desire of being approved, deliver me, Jesus.[7]

---

6. For a contemporary example of Jesus-infused meekness I propose the South African Anglican cleric and theologian, Bishop Tutu. He is known for his work as an anti-apartheid and human rights activist. His book, *Bishop Desmond Tutu: The Voice of One Crying in the Wilderness*, would be a good place to begin.

7. Wiget, "One-Scary-to-Pray-Prayer."

Ravenous for Righteousness

Blessed are those who hunger and thirst for righteousness, for they shall be filled.

—MATT 5:6

Jesus wants to save us from religiously sanctioned despair, the kind that doesn't believe the world can be made better, the kind that either blatantly or subtly teaches people to just be quiet and behave and wait for something big to happen someday.

—ROB BELL[1]

AS WE'VE BEEN SAYING, it's not a good idea to amputate these "Blessed Attitudes" from the rest of the Sermon as if they were an appendage. They represent the rich soil in which the Christlike life grows. Each one signifies a nutrient essential for a healthy and fruitful kingdom life. We come now to the fourth blessed nutrient: *a craving to do what is right.*

In our trajectory into Christlike-ness you might notice a turning point here. When we recognize our poverty of spirit, we mourn over it and develop a meek spirit as a result. But true followers of Jesus are not content to settle down there. With the Spirit's aid, we work up an appetite to become better human beings on a quest to make the world a better place. *We're dying to be more and more like Jesus!*

I was teaching a Bible study with a group of recovering alcoholics and drug addicts. I can't remember feeding a group of people hungrier for

---

1. Bell and Golden, *Jesus Wants to Save Christians*, 172.

change. Each of the men in the program have hit bottom in their addiction and are quite clear about their spiritual poverty. They mourn their former choices, are humbled by the grace that offers them a second chance, and are *ravenous for righteousness*.

This is the first of seven times Jesus uses the word "righteousness" in the address. In one place he tells us that the sort of righteousness that defines his kingdom is that which qualitatively "surpasses the righteousness of the Pharisees and teachers of the law," without which we're hard-pressed to "enter" the kingdom, let alone *advance* it.

Jesus didn't come here with a fistful of *Religion Redux*; instead, he explained a whole new way of behaving that starts on the inside and shows up on the outside. Any sort of "tacked on" righteousness simply will not do. We can try to hook "good works" onto our branches like ornaments on a Christmas tree, but they tend to drop off as the tree rots. Alternatively, he injects healthy sap into our roots, which courses through our branches and produces a harvest of good fruit.

Since righteousness begins when "self" is crucified,[2] the harvest is no monument to self-effort. "Some people will be virtuous not because they love God's will," says Thomas Merton, "but because they want to admire their own virtues."[3] Yet when rooted in the blessed attitudes, righteousness can safely take place without threat of being sucked into self-aggrandizement. "Nothing is more beautiful than righteousness and nothing is more hideous than self-righteousness."[4]

What's in It for Us?

> Be especially careful when you are trying to be good so that you don't make a performance out of it. It might be good theater, but the God who made you won't be applauding. (Matt 6:1, The Message Bible)

"It is possible for a man to be self-centered in his self-denial and self-righteous in his self-sacrifice," preached Martin Luther King. "He may be generous in order to feed his ego and pious in order to feed his pride. Man has the tragic capacity to relegate a heightening virtue to a tragic vice. Without

---

2. Gal 2:20.
3. Merton, *New Seeds of Contemplation*, 75.
4. Jones, *Unshakable Kingdom*, 143.

love, benevolence becomes egotism, and martyrdom becomes spiritual pride."[5]

Some believers hunger for a righteousness that promises earthly rewards, but the better reward—whether in the hereafter or the here and now—is to live the best version of ourselves while enjoying intimacy with the Rewarder himself. The most exquisite rewards are those that come from living so near him that you feel his heart beating inside your chest and hear his whisper in your ear.

While *lawligans* do righteousness as image-management and to feel good about themselves, those pursuing *surpassing righteousness* merely hope to reflect glory back to God and advance his kingship on earth. They don't use God to make themselves look good, but revel in the privilege of being used by him to show others how good he is!

We do our best work in secret, in one-handed transactions.[6] We only require one hand to reach into our pocket to hand a gift over to someone in need. It takes two hands to dole out our donation with one and record it in a ledger with the other. But love doesn't keep books or think in terms of profit and loss any more than a mother records the number of times she heats her baby's bottle or changes its diaper.

Over the next few chapters we'll talk about righteousness and rules, how righteousness is meant for the common good, how it's rooted in what we call "The Golden Rule," and how righteous people pray. Oh, and then I'll ask you to ask yourself how hungry you are for that brand of righteousness.

---

5. King, "Paul's Letter to American Christians," para. 25.
6. Matt 6:3.

Better Rules ≠ Better Lives

You have heard it said . . . But I say . . .
—MATT 5:21, 27, 33, 38

The Sermon on the Mount is not a set of rules and regulations: it is a statement of the life we will live when the Holy Spirit is getting his way with us.

—OSWALD CHAMBERS[1]

THE CORROSIVE INFLUENCE OF pop culture and political tribalism has pilfered the plot, made off with the original narrative of rightness (or righteousness if you prefer), and sells it to people who demand a superstar role. In contrast to artery-clogging comfort food, this righteousness is a nutritious meal for which our innermost being hungers. It digs deeper than symptom-treating behavior modification and wends its way into the heart of the matter.

The Spirit excavates down to the root of our egocentric self and weeds out its seeds before they have an opportunity to germinate. In his Sermon, Jesus addresses the reasons for murder, marital infidelity, and mendacity. He confronts their concealed toxic motivations before they grow up into sprawling orchards bearing noxious fruit that sickens its consumers.

Righteousness rooted in rules revolves around particular sinful activities. Whereas Jesus begins with the kind of internal *attitudes that lead to actions*. In his *beatitudinal* modus operandi, motives and deeds are

---

1. Chambers, *My Utmost for His Highest*, 96.

inseparable, for together they produce healthier fruit than any external code of dos and don'ts.[2]

In order to help us imagine righteousness in real time Jesus provides us with a number of case studies that demonstrate his superior route to right living. He calls our attention to some of the golden oldies—laws against murder, adultery, lying, violence, and revenge. It's not an exhaustive list of "no-no's," any more than Moses' famous list of ten could be said to cover every moral issue of concern to God. These case studies of kingdom life are *illustrative* rather than *comprehensive*. He proposes several imaginative examples and calls us to apply the principles therein every day in a multitude of ways.

These case studies are best seen as illustrations of the trajectory of the kingdom-hearted person. He beckons us into a way of living from the inside out without spelling out exactly what to do in the particular scenarios he posits. These are not directives that point us to the precise way to treat an adversary on our way to court or how to measure out the exact distance to carry someone else's backpack for them.

These vignettes don't cover all the misbehaviors by which we're tempted. And he makes no attempt to address every loophole or fill every pothole. We could obey each command to the letter and still find ways to hate and hurt one another.

God gave the Jews a number of *prescriptions* (laws) to protect their unity as a nation until Jesus came to take over the people-changing business. He followed God's prescriptions to a "T" and bore the consequences we deserved for ignoring them. Now in place of *prescriptions* we have a *Person*—an indwelling, resurrected, empowering Person who flips the script from "You have heard it said . . ." to "But I say . . ." He wasn't trying to improve on the old *prescription*; instead, he becomes our live-in Savior enabling us to live the way he originally intended.

Surpassing righteousness is not, as we might suspect, a more *stringent righteousness*, but an entirely different approach to it. It's the counternarrative to legalism. It begins with a gift of imputed righteousness (justification) and grows into an inside-out demonstration of it (sanctification).

---

2. This is not to imply that there are no "dos and don'ts" in the Jesus way. Some people try to concoct their own version of the faith apart from all don'ts. But as our Good Shepherd, for our own good, the good of others, and for his glory, he warns us to avoid toxic behaviors. His don'ts in this Sermon alone are many: *Don't swear, don't turn someone away who has needs, don't practice revenge, don't do the disciplines for human accolades, don't judge, don't live for Mammon, don't worry about tomorrow . . .* You get the point.

PART TWO | UTTERLY UPSIDE-DOWN ATTITUDES

Incurably religious people hunger and thirst for more laws, better guardrails to keep them from acting on their self-indulgent impulses. Avid rule-keepers fill themselves with more of themselves rather than filling up on the Spirit. "As noble as our intentions might be, the less space God has to operate until he is finally pushed out altogether and all we are left with is ourselves and our own inadequate attempts at righteousness."[3]

I recently visited an old friend who lives way out at the end of a Northern California country road. As I got out of my car and approached his house, I eyed an enormous Saint Bernard sitting in the shade of a great old oak tree. More importantly, I noticed him noticing me. As they are the ones you always see in photos at the ready with a small keg of brandy fastened to their collars for the random fallen skier, I was under the impression that this particular brand of canine is always laid-back and human friendly. I abandoned that impression at first snarl. This animal was no "saint"!

Though he outweighed me by a great deal he lumbered toward me faster than I retreated. Just as he lunged for me, I screamed like a little girl, so claimed my friend. (I'm pretty sure he made that part up.) Anyhow, as the creature rose to his hind legs the industrial strength chain that held him fast to the sturdy old tree trunk stopped him cold and all but broke his neck in the process!

Religious rule-keepers are those who depend on laws, like chains, to hold back their ferocious nature. The chains don't turn their evil predispositions into something good—from vicious pit bulls into gentle collies—they just restrain them from doing more harm than good. It's the strength of the chain, not the nature of the dog, that keeps them in check.

Jesus didn't come to upgrade the rules by giving us a bigger chain; instead, he transforms our nature into something increasingly better. It's that transformation for which we must hunger and thirst most.

---

3. McBrayer, *Jesus Tribe*, 70.

Righteousness for the Common Good

Injustice anywhere is a threat to justice everywhere. We are caught in an inescapable network of mutuality, tied in a single garment of destiny. Whatever affects one directly affects all indirectly.

—MARTIN LUTHER KING JR.[1]

Blessed are those who hunger and thirst for righteousness, for they shall be filled.

—MATT 5:6

FIVE ENGLISH VERSIONS OF this verse render "righteousness" as "justice." Others say we are to hunger "for what is right" or "to see right prevail." Jesus has on his mind a surpassing righteousness that includes both *personal holiness* and *public justice*. He invites us to concern ourselves with all that concerns him, including nurturing his image in every person at every stage of life, creation care, equitable economic policies, and speaking up for the most vulnerable and marginalized.

If not directly, then by inference most of my early pastors and teachers had a fissure in their concept of righteousness, which they bequeathed to me. I was mentored in a theological system, complete with proof texts for their prejudiced notions that all but eliminated social justice in favor of an exclusive emphasis on personal piety—as though one could exist without the other.

---

1. MLK's letter from the Birmingham, Alabama jail in 1963

PART TWO | UTTERLY UPSIDE-DOWN ATTITUDES

The Greek term used throughout the New Testament for righteousness (*dikaiosune*) includes both personal and public applications. Jesus preached a multidimensional holistic rightness where individual piety and social justice are not mutually exclusive, but symbiotic impulses in the Christ follower's heart.

Those Jesus calls "blessed" are as famished for restorative justice as they are for personal virtue, for these are merely two aspects of the same thing. Put another way: *Justice is righteousness for the common good.*[2]

He want us to hunger for God's justice because the hungry need justice. "The hungry are hungry for food and for the justice that would right the imbalances that keep them hungry."[3]

Many Christians are hungrier to *have a better life* for themselves than to *lead a better life* for the glory of God and the good of others—let alone to *leave a better world* than the one they inherited. They savor *shalom* for themselves and their tribe but are slow to share it outside their own cultural, racial, and geopolitical boundaries. The peace they experience "passes understanding" yet fails to *pass over* to people outside their social class or national borders. A ninth-century French author wrote to her son telling him that hungering for God's righteousness means "making just laws, not taking advantage of the poor, and rendering legal judgments with mercy."[4]

Since Jesus loathes injustice, his followers will hunger for justice to be dispensed wherever they detect its absence. They will "seek first the Kingdom and its justice"[5] not only for themselves but for others whose presence is ignored and their pleas for help are unheeded. When they see justice being held at bay it's a cue to pray and to take action for the common good.

It should be clear to us by now that though God wills an end of hunger and poverty, we'll have to wait for it to be *fully realized* at the second coming of the Lord Jesus. "Secure on that solid rock, we will plunge into this unjust world, changing now all we can and knowing that the risen King will complete the victory at his glorious return."[6]

2. The Hebrew Bible often places the two terms ("righteousness and justice") side by side, while the New Testament employs one word to encompass them both. The context in each passage determines which of the two is being addressed, if not both at the same time.

3. Eklund, *Beatitudes through the Ages*, 250.

4. Eklund, *Beatitudes through the Ages*, 43.

5. A legitimate translation of Matt 6:33.

6. Sider, *Rich Christians*, 45.

Good Christians of the eighteenth and nineteenth centuries formed the backbone of the abolition movements in Britain and America, and provided the moral and political support for social reform that improved the lives of women, prisoners, children, the mentally ill, and other marginalized groups. Wheaton College even served as a stop on the Underground Railroad, and to this day, most of the organizations fighting human trafficking are faith-based.

Our nation's founders claimed a "self-evident" truth that all humans are equal and that our Creator has endowed us with "certain unalienable Rights." (These "Rights" were so important to the writers of the Declaration that they capitalized the word.) Pursuing a just distribution of those rights makes one a good American as well as a faithful follower of Christ.[7]

Achieving this *common-good righteousness* requires more than abstaining from murder or fornication or punching people in the face. Jesus drills down further into our attitudinal control center and reveals the damage we do when we disparage our neighbors' inherent worth. He draws a causal line from devaluing fellow image bearers to murder. Murder begins in the killer's *heart* before he forms a plan in his *head* and eventually perpetrates it with his *hands*.

Kingdom subversives have an appetite for something much better, not only for what nourishes them personally but also for that which enriches their neighbors. They "seek first" this kingdom's righteousness for themselves and justice for those who lack their own agency and opportunity. They think, talk, act, vote, and advocate *for the common good.*

---

7. While some people conflate their preferred party's platform with their tribe's exclusive right to righteousness, political alliances are virtually useless in our definition and demonstration of Jesus' surpassing righteousness. His idea of what is right is transcultural, whereas parties and platforms are fickle and tend to die slow deaths.

"Rhodium" Rule Righteousness

So in everything, do to others what you would have them do to you, for this sums up the Law and the Prophets.

—Matt 7:12

What a difference it would make in our economic system if the employer would treat every employee as he would like to be treated as an employee, if he would give every girl the wage he would like his daughter to have were she an employee; in our race relationships if we treated people of color as we would like to be treated if we were born with their same skin pigmentation.

—E. Stanley Jones[1]

This has to be the most familiar and frequently quoted line in all of Jesus' teachings. In it he sums up the plot of not only his Sermon, but his entire mission. This is what he's all about! What would you like other people to do to you? Jesus says: *Don't wait; do it to them!*

Though commonly known as the "Golden Rule," I suggest it's more like *Rhodium* (ˈrōdēəm), which is the rarest of metals on the planet. Though I doubt my new label for it will catch on, my point is that the actual practice of Jesus' rule is as rare and valuable as this rare metal. You have to look high and low to excavate even the tiniest samples of it among humans.

---

1. Jones, *Unshakable Kingdom*, 139.
   It's worth noting that Jones, as a missionary in India, dealt with a severe caste system wherein the upper classes and under classes never mixed.

"Rhodium" Rule Righteousness

Wendell Berry rephrased it: "Do unto those downstream as you would have those upstream do unto you." We all have someone *downstream* to us, people that are affected by our actions or lack thereof. Problem is, we often either don't realize it or we simply don't care.

Power corrupts and privilege is blind. If *power* is the ultimate stimulant, *privilege* is the most common anesthesia. Most of us are so accustomed to whatever advantages we may have that we're tone deaf to our less fortunate neighbors. As someone said, "Privilege is when you think something is not a problem because it's not a problem to you personally."

Challenging people's privilege is a risky business. Just ask Jesus who was executed for this very *crime* against the Jewish aristocracy and Roman occupying forces! Furthermore, he warned his followers that if they chose the same subversive path they would be treated likewise. And they were.

Most of us are so used to having all the toys at our disposal that we get peeved when required to share them with other kids in the class. That's more than selfishness; it's entitled privilege. We have the choice to exploit it for our own advantage or, as the Rule commands, steward it to the advantage of our less prosperous neighbors.

In reference to the privilege of one ethnic group over another, Greg Boyd says, "The majority of white people don't 'get it.' What's worse, [they] don't know that they don't 'get it.' Worst of all, [they] don't really know that there's anything to 'get.'"[2] I would add that the only thing worse is when they refuse to get what is staring them in the face and then swear up and down that there's nothing *to* get!

As far *downstream* as you may be, there's always someone further down—people with less social, economic, and cultural capital than you. Kingdom people treat such people as though our roles were reversed and we were the ones below them on the social register. If you were the poorest person in your neighborhood, the least educated, the most socially backward, wouldn't you wish to be treated with the respect that befits our shared humanity?

Jesus ups the ante when he says in another place, "Inasmuch as you've done it to one of the least of these my brothers, you've done it to me."[3] Treating your neighbor as you want to be treated is one thing, but seeing Jesus *in your neighbor*, especially your hungry, thirsty, ill-clothed, or unhoused

---

2. Boyd, "Why Whites Have Trouble," para. 1.
3. Matt 25:40.

neighbor, is another thing altogether. Treating Jesus well requires that we treat our under-served, underclass neighbors with love and respect.

We all have people *upstream* from us as well—those who have more cash or clout, more agency and opportunity than we have. Those who use their power to exploit us can be some of the most difficult to love. Those who disrespect us with the back of their hand may very well be God's gift to us to test our capacity to love unconditionally—a test I seem to have to take over and over again!

"You can't walk straight when you hate," preached Martin Luther King. "You can't stand upright. Your vision is distorted."[4] Hating them just turns us into them. The harm we wish on them usually boomerangs back on us.

"Haters want us to hate them because hate is incapacitating. When we hate, we can't operate from our real selves, which is our strength."[5] Jesus instructs us how to deprive the haters of their objective by refusing to fall into their lair.

Prejudicial grouping of people highlights inherent distinctions between them based on externals like skin hue, social standing, language, culture, politics, or economics. All of these are superficial distinguishers. According to David Brooks, "If you see other people as souls, it's much harder to loathe groups of them."

The Nazi-sanctioned Bishop, Ludwig Müller sank so low as to retranslate the Sermon on the Mount in keeping with his xenophobic values. He has Jesus saying such things as: "Happy are those who are at peace with their fellow Germans . . . Do not remain unreconciled to the fellow member of your own people . . . " To Müller, love of neighbor meant loving only German neighbors. History shows that if you can limit the definition of "neighbor" to anyone non-foreign, you can rationalize any harmful behavior against anyone that you categorize as the "other."

"Othering" people dehumanizes them by dividing and reducing them to categories—"those Mexicans" or "those Muslims" or "those homeless." It's a convenient way to ignore whole populations and avoid actual engagement with individuals outside our own socioeconomic or ethnic identity. It is much harder to caricature and classify people when you look them in the eye, hear their voice, and shake their hand.

We take the first step in the direction of the kind of righteousness that outshines and outstrips its artificial versions when we decline to pigeonhole

---

4. King, "Loving Your Enemies," para. 22.
5. Lamott, *Almost Everything*, 75.

people in conveniently labeled boxes and begin to love them based on our commonality. "The opposite of Othering is not saming,'" says John A. Powell, "it is belonging. And belonging does not insist that we are all the same. It means we recognize and celebrate our differences, in a society where 'we the people' includes all the people."[6]

"The Rule" sums up Jesus' Address and possibly all of his teachings. It's the mantra for God's new society, the oft-repeated refrain in the Christian anthem. It reveals the way that Jesus' kingship burrows itself into how we do relationships, manage our resources, formulate our politics, and resist the temptation to exploit one another for our own gain.

Maybe we call it "Golden" (or Rhodium) because of how much it costs us to obey it. Only those ravenous for righteousness, those who are *dying to be like Jesus*, will make discernible progress in its direction!

---

6. Powell, "Us vs Them," para. 20.

How Righteous Rebels Pray

When you pray . . .

—MATT 6:5

The call to prayer, an act that drags egotism into the open and begins to do something about it, is a major corrective to the political problems of the day. . . . As our loyalties are detached from nation, club, race or other affiliation, our actual capacity for community increases.

—EUGENE PETERSON[1]

OF THE THREE EXAMPLES of doing *righteousness for the right reasons*: giving, fasting, and prayer, Jesus' teaching on the latter is the most familiar and contains history's most often recited petition.

The prayer we call "The Lord's Prayer" is one of Jesus' extra-strength prescriptions for turning the world upside down. This is how those who are hungry and thirsty to see the world righted pray. Prayer is one of the chief ways we contend for the advance of the rule of God on earth and "the renewal of all things."[2]

Were a Roman official to eavesdrop on early kingdom-hungry Christians praying like this, they would have hightailed it to HQ to report them as seditious troublemakers! Rome's rule depended on a compliant citizenry, and this prayer incites anything but compliance. "The Lord's Prayer is also

---

1. Peterson, *Where Your Treasure Is*, 14.
2. Matt 19:28.

a political manifesto" wherein "we are seeking, supporting, and desiring another kingdom and asking the king to bring it to fruition."[3]

"Be careful how you pray," wrote E. Stanley Jones. "You may be the answer."[4]

Let's do a quick scan of the contents of this famous prayer and offer some simple ways to apply it.

"Our Father in Heaven . . . "

You'll notice the plural pronouns interwoven throughout: "*Our* Father. . . . Give *us our* daily bread. . . . Forgive *us*. . . . As *we* forgive. . . . Deliver *us*. . . . " Evidently, Jesus meant his prayer to be prayed (if not word for word, concept for concept) in harmony with other people. If not actually in the company of others, we pray it in *solidarity* with the rest of Christ's body worldwide. At any given moment people all over the planet are praying the prayer of the Lord, if not verbatim, at least with the same general ingredients according to the dietary need of the hour.

This prayer isn't only about *me* and *my* needs, but *us* and *our* needs. Jesus imagined us thinking beyond *just us* in order to intercede for *justice* to "roll on like a river and righteousness like a never-failing stream!" (Amos 5:24).

> Oh Father, we're all derived from you. As bearers of your image and partakers of your nature we are members of the same human family. With this family we make these requests along with and on behalf of one another.

"Hallowed Be Your Name . . . "

We hallow no name but his. There is only one Person to whom this exclusive respect is due, and it isn't Caesar or any other world leader, entertainer, athlete, artist, or scholar.

> Ours is a paltry reflection of your renown. What you receive back from your redeemed and your unredeemed children is an immeasurably inadequate representation of all you are due. From the

---

3. Schiess, *Liturgy of Politics*, 142.
4. Jones, *Song of Ascents*, 118.

worst to the best of us, Lord, you are worthy of more! Get glory for yourself in our hearts, homes, and homelands.

"Your Kingdom Come, Your Will Be Done . . ."

In Jesus' day, under Roman law this could have been construed as treason, which was one of the "crimes" for which he was ultimately executed.

The mob shouted at Pilate, "Anyone who claims to be a king opposes Caesar!"[5] Thessalonian antagonizers roared about the invasion of their town by Jesus followers: "They have caused trouble all over the world . . . are defying Caesar's decrees, saying that there is another king, one called Jesus."[6] There wasn't room in the Empire for two kings. Jesus and his mischief-making followers were a threat to business as usual in the Empire.

Though it may not typically be the spirit in which it is recited today in most of our comfy sanctuaries, hungry early adopters of the prayer pled for God's will to counter the will of Caesar and his cronies. To pray it rightly is to seek God's will to realign earth with heaven. "Faith without works is dead. Prayer without work is hypocrisy. Unless we actively work to build for God's kingdom, the Lord's Prayer—'Your kingdom come'—is a lie on our lips."[7]

In a sense, all prayer is a *subversive* act, as it challenges unjust systems and dethrones the "rulers of the darkness of this world" that animate those systems. Those who pray with hunger for righteousness recognize how the singular rule of the "King of all other kings and Lord of all other lords" subverts the rule of anti-kingdom systems and lays the groundwork for God's new society on earth.

> Come, Benevolent Ruler, and take your rightful throne in our hearts, in our churches, in our courts, and in our culture. Come, Lord, and make the kingdoms of this world become more and more the Kingdom of our Lord and of his Christ!

---

5. John 19:12.
6. Acts 17:6–7.
7. Arnold, *Prayer God Answers*, 38.

"On Earth as It Is in Heaven . . . "

Our requests are not mere abstract notions. We want the King and his ways to influence life here *on earth,* often with tangible consequences. We can't rightly pray this without letting God have his way in how we manage our resources and time in order to improve the world.

We don't pray that he will *uproot* us from earth and *repot* us in heaven so we can begin to bloom. Instead, we pray that heaven's seedlings will be planted in our hearts, homes, and communities to grow into fruit-bearing trees that feed the nations.

Though it won't happen fully until Jesus returns and heaven descends on earth again, our prayer is that heaven's *perfection* will gradually replace earth's *dysfunction.*

"Prayer enhances our skills of citizenry—our commitments, our involvements, our values, our passion for social justice."[8]

> Our ways are not yours, Oh Lord, and they're killing our personal lives, our justice systems (so-called), and the planet over which you've made us stewards. Bring heaven's life here to earth and let us partner with you in the doing of it!

"Give Us This Day Our Daily Bread . . . "

A lot of people say they're "starving" when they miss lunch, while most of the world lives on less than $2 a day. The prayer of the poor for daily bread is more desperate than mine. "While dependence on God is our eternal reality," says Kaitlyn Schiess, "we are awaiting the end of the current reality of scarcity in some places and extravagance in others, of some who grasp for crumbs while others hoard resources."[9] When we pray, we do so in solidarity with all our neighbors for a more equitable distribution of food and funds.

While your refrigerator might be full of groceries, you have neighbors (near and far) who, for one reason or another, aren't as fortunate. Since the poor reside in God's heart, his stealthy way of inserting them into our hearts is by sneaking them into our prayers. We make our requests in

---

8. Peterson, *Where Your Treasure Is,* 42.
9. Schiess, *Liturgy of Politics,* 97.

solidarity with all those who go to bed (if they even have a bed) with empty stomachs.[10]

> Lord, we identify with our truly starving image-bearing human family members around the globe and ask you to put food on our collective table. May no one in the world go to bed hungry tonight. Include us as part of the solution and teach us to share our bread with those who have none.

"Forgive Us Our Trespasses . . ."

Was it by design that he brought up our need for forgiveness right after the prayer for daily bread?

Could he be suggesting that we need forgiveness for trespassing in our neighbors' kitchen and eating the bread that was meant for them?

Is our apathy about world hunger and our greed to hold on to what is "ours" at issue in this request for forgiveness?

Of course, we trespass in many other ways than this, but given that God's will boils down loving our neighbor, second only to loving him, maybe he's asking us to consider how we consume more than our share at the expense of those who already possess too little. "Oh, America," wrote Martin Luther King Jr., "how often have you taken necessities from the masses to give luxuries to the classes?"[11]

Maybe Jesus was pointing out our self-indulgence and pointing us toward a generous and more equitable distribution of anything that human flourishing requires.

> Forgive us, Lord, for all we've done and not done that hurts your heart and harms our fellow travelers. Forgive us for accumulating and consuming more than our share.

---

10. It is estimated that over 60 percent of the 50,000 agencies working with food banks nationwide are faith-based organizations. I've personally been involved with a few of them myself and can attest to their viability. Other examples of faith-based organizations that focus on addressing food insecurity include World Vision, Bread for the World, Food for the Hungry, World Hunger Relief Inc., Compassion International, and Samaritan's Purse.

11. King, "Paul's Letter to American Churches," para. 12.

"As We Forgive Those Who Trespass against Us . . . "

This might be the most countercultural part of the prayer. Revenge is the way of the jungle. Forgive? Are you crazy? God can, but not I!

We withhold forgiveness to "maintain our sense of superiority," says Richard Rohr. "Non-forgiveness is a form of power over another person, a way to manipulate, shame, control and diminish another."[12] Forgiving those who abuse their power drains the bile we've accumulated in our hearts.

We need forgiveness for trespassing and stealing someone else's bread, and we need to forgive trespassers for stealing ours.

> Knowing that forgiveness makes the whole world a better place to live, we forgive, Lord. We won't let our enemies control us by hating them. We release them from our judgment and leave the judging to you.

"Lead Us Not into Temptation but Deliver Us from Evil."

Forgiveness for our bad behavior isn't all we need. Those who truly hunger for righteousness are hungry to avoid repeat performances of sinful behavior. In order to veer away from self-destructive and socially toxic behaviors and to run toward a more *shalom*-centered society, we need God's help.

We're told repeatedly to love our neighbors as ourselves, though we're never commanded to love ourselves. As it is our default position we don't need a command for that. On the other hand, loving others requires some effort. Possibly our greatest temptation and most stubborn evil from which we need to be freed is loving ourselves *instead of* our neighbors.

> Lord, lead us away from the temptation to love only ourselves and free us from attitudes and behaviors that diminish *shalom* in our own souls and in the soul of our culture.

"Yours Is the Kingdom, the Power and the Glory"

The *kingdom* we pray to "come" and the "will" we yearn to see "done" is God's. It's his right to rule the planet and the people on it.

---

12. Rohr, *Jesus' Plan*, 79.

For his kingdom to descend, for bread to be equitably distributed, for forgiveness to be enjoyed and shared, and for our release from Satan's snares, his more-than-sufficient *power* is required.

The end game, the ultimate goal of it all—in fact, the mother of all goals—is *the glory of God*. The renown of his Person, the advance of his rule, and the renewal of his original plan for earth all point to the outshining of his splendor!

> Lord, since everything belongs to you, you have the right and the power to manage your kingdom in any way you choose, all of which radiates with your unique splendor! Amen.

❊ ❊ ❊

A Quick Word about Fasting for the Common Good

> When you fast, do not look somber as the hypocrites do, for they disfigure their faces to show others they are fasting. (Matt 6:16)

One final example of Jesus' *righteousness for the right reasons* is the spiritual discipline of fasting. One fasts when hungrier for righteousness and justice than for food.

Fasting can be as much about "giving to the needy"[13] as it is about deepening one's own spiritual life. Many of the early Christians fasted at times so they would have enough to feed those who came to their door for help. Due to their own poverty, they would otherwise have had to send them away hungry. Gregory the Great said that "a man fasts not to God but to himself, if he does not give to the poor what he denies his belly for a time, but reserves it to be given to his belly later."[14]

Similarly, when unexpected guests knocked on the Catholic Worker Center door in New York City, Dorothy Day used to say as she welcomed them in, "There's always enough for one more. Everyone just takes a little less." One reason for fasting is to take a little less so that we will have a little more to share.

---

13. Isa 58:6–7. Some call this practice of voluntary fasting in order to supply the needs of others as "social fasting."

14. As quoted in Schiess, *Liturgy of Politics*, 94.

If fasting involves taking a little less from the refrigerator for yourself, mightn't it also apply to taking a little less stuff we don't need from Walmart, Nordstrom, and Honest John's Used Car Lot? If we all fasted our over-indulgence, got off the consumerist gerbil wheel and lived a little more simply, we could certainly give more to those with less.

How Hungry? How Thirsty?

Blessed are those who hunger and thirst for righteousness, for they shall be filled.

—Matt 5:6

Every Christian will become at last what their desires have made them. We are all the sum total of our hungers.

—A. W. Tozer

The kind of surpassing *righteousness* Jesus prescribes involves a daily dying to everything for which our lower selves clamor. The life he invites us into involves lugging around a heavy piece of lumber designed for nothing short of execution of that lower self. Fortunately, this execution is routinely followed by resurrection!

Seeking the kingdom "first" doesn't mean getting it out of the way so we can feel good about ourselves going ahead and seeking a bunch of other stuff of our own choosing. By "first," Jesus means seek it above all else, first in priority, the sort of priority that remains first and influences every lesser priority.

He claims that sometimes the price of transformation calls for plucking out a wandering eye or amputating an unruly limb.[1] Hyperbole notwithstanding, it's clear that righteousness doesn't come by accident. Sometimes we just have to remove the cause of temptation and proceed maimed in man's sight in order to be whole in God's.

1. Matt 5:29–30.

How Hungry? How Thirsty?

Many Christians want to make some improvements in select areas of their lives. This usually amounts to something more like a *wish* than a hunger. Jesus calls for an all-consuming craving for more than a series of minor adjustments, but a serious incremental transformation until our person and purpose more closely resemble his.

Few of us will ever know real hunger or thirst. We use expressions like, "I'm starving!" or "I'm dying of thirst!" But for most of us the experience will never approach starvation. Nor will our temporary lack of hydration be fatal. To Jesus, hunger and thirst was something more than what we feel when we miss lunch or forget to bring our mineral water to work.

Protein and water were in short supply for most of those in his audience that day. They had no corner stores to pick up a quick snack to tide them over till dinner. With the absence of kitchen faucets and bottled water by the case, they had to make the trek to the river or the town well. They knew from experience the kind of hunger and thirst that Jesus said would yield righteousness. "This Beatitude is for those who desire righteousness as a matter of life and death. . . . The great barrier to our becoming fully Christian is our failure to desire it enough, our deep-rooted unwillingness to pay the price of it, our fundamental desire not to upset life, but to keep it as it is."[2]

Some are hungrier for *blessedness* than for *righteousness*. They waste their hunger pangs on paltry pursuits like economic abundance, acquisition of power, or climbing the social ladder. But the pursuit of blessing for its own sake yields neither blessedness nor righteousness.

How can he fill us if we're already full of ourselves, saturated with our accomplishments, and glutted with our possessions? Though we may claim to be hungry for righteousness, the reality is we have little stomach for what it requires to be like Jesus.

Sometimes it takes starving ourselves of less nourishing alternatives to jumpstart our system and to initiate a craving for what genuinely feeds our soul. Fasting food or media or various forms of entertainment may increase our hunger for what matters.

"Take a taste," says David, "and see for yourself that the Lord is good" (Ps 34:8).[3]

---

2. Barclay, *Beatitudes*, 50.

3. I can think of no person hungrier for righteousness and justice than the inimitable prophet, pastor, and author: A. W. Tozer. Of the dozens of books he wrote I'd suggest any of these: *The Pursuit of God, God's Pursuit of Man, The Root of the Righteous, The Knowledge of the Holy,* or the biography of his life, *A. W. Tozer: A Passion for God.*

Have Mercy—Will Travel

(The Beneficiaries and Benefactors of Mercy)

Blessed are the merciful for they shall obtain mercy.
—Matt 6:7

The quality of mercy is not strain'd,
It droppeth as the gentle rain from heaven
Upon the place beneath: it is twice blest;
It blesseth him that gives and him that takes"
—The Bard[1]

OF THE EIGHT QUALITIES that we refer to as "Beatitudes," *mercy* stands out like an orchid in the fall. Among all his attributes, mercy is one of the Lord's most alluring and is central to the way we experience and express his life. He wants to so fill us with heaven's mercy that we become, as he is, "mercy-full" in all our earthly interactions. We who have filled up on mercy, like the disciples after feeding the five thousand, find ourselves with baskets full of leftovers.

Having already been "mercied," the merciful are poised to show mercy to others, forming a continuous loop of mercy to mercy. The more

---

1. From *The Merchant of Venice*, 4.1

heaven-sent mercy we gratefully receive, the more we'll be able to give on earth. It's "twice blest." It "blesseth him that gives and him that takes."

As we've been saying, these qualities are not independent of the rest of the Sermon as *hors d'oeuvres* to hold us over for the main course. They're more than a mere list of advisable virtues to whet our appetite for the real meat of his message. These blessed attitudes do more than serve as a succinct description of the Jesus-shaped life; they invite us *into* that life. They act as portals through which we enter and begin to engage with him and with the rest of his magnificent teaching.

There is an intentional sequence in these from being *poor in spirit* all the way to being *persecuted* for our faith. When emptied of our illusion of superiority, grieving it, being humbled by it, and working up an appetite for a substantive righteousness, we find ourselves desiring to mature in *mercy*. Righteousness unmodified by mercy is Pharisaical and sour-visaged. But when it is planted in mercy-fertilized soil it produces fruit for the famished.

If not for mercy we would never have gotten to the starting line in the first place. It's what qualifies us to enter the race, mends our hobbled natures so we can run all the way to the finish, and induces in us the will to help other runners along the way.

Sometimes people become *righteously rigid* after entering the race. Having forgotten that they were "mercied" into it to begin with, rather than helping other runners in their leg of the race, they sprint right past them without even noticing their hobbled fellow runners.

Mercy-blessed runners know that their progress is not due to their discipline or superior genetics. Hard work and good genes don't tell the whole story of their spiritual success. Those most familiar with God's mercy become wellsprings of it to those most in need.

As with all the Beatitudes, no one is better at this than Jesus. If you want to be like him, be merciful.

Let's take the following chapters to unpack this essential quality of mercy. We'll discuss how mercy and justice are inextricably linked and how it is best identified as an action as opposed to an abstraction. We'll go on to show how the merciful defy an idolatrous relationship with money, refuse to be duped by money-grabbing preachers, and resist the lure of worry over material sufficiency.

Justice, Mercy's Sibling

Central to the way of Jesus is serving, which is the loving use of whatever power you possess for the good of another.
—Rob Bell[1]

THOUGH OFTEN SET IN opposition to each other by Bible readers, *mercy* and *justice* actually share the same DNA. As there is an intentional sequence to the blessed attitudes, it's no coincidence that Jesus set the blessedness of the *merciful* right after *hungering for justice.*

The prophet links the two in his abridged version of what the Lord requires: "to act justly, love mercy and to walk humbly with God" (Mic 6:8). I've often thought if there were such a thing as a *New American Dream Version of the Bible* Micah's requirements might look more like: *Seek justice for yourself, demand mercy from others, and expect them to walk humbly with your God.* I like the NIV better!

Wendell Berry says: "Rats and roaches live by competition under the laws of supply and demand; it is the privilege of human beings to live under the laws of justice and mercy." The merciful favor and work toward the elimination of everything that keeps *shalom* at bay on earth: injustice, poverty, disease, and the spiritual powers that inspire them.

Those who are full of *mercy* are well known for caring deeply about *justice* for those who have little to no way of acquiring it for themselves. Moses (Deut 10:17–18), David (Ps 103:6), Solomon (Prov 29:7), Isaiah (Isa 1:17), Amos (Amos 5:24), James (Jas 1:27), and many other Bible authors all agree with Jesus that *the just are merciful and the merciful are just.*

---

1. Bell and Golden, *Jesus Wants to Save Christians,* 86.

Justice, Mercy's Sibling

Justice restores the community to the way God envisioned it in the beginning. For those who aren't allergic to the phrase, let's call it "social justice." (Before you slam the book closed or throw your Kindle against the wall, "social" is simply a modifier to clarify that we're not talking about justice for "just us," as in you and me.) The justice that God calls for is for "Us" (the universal "Us," i.e., all of us).

Mercy-filled people not only feel the pain of others but are moved to action in an effort to relieve their suffering. They work to renew the world in keeping with the model bequeathed to us by Jesus. Our work will be complete when he returns to join heaven and earth. In the meantime, our mercy-filled lives are previews of coming attractions!

The other word that many Christians have a severe reaction to is—wait for it—"Politics!"

The term itself comes from *polis*, the Greek word for "people." Therefore, politics is simply what we say and do for the sake of *people* in hopes of creating the best possible society for the good of all. I admit it's a messy business; however, according to Peter Wehner politics is "an imperfect but essential way to advance justice and human flourishing . . . if Christians care about justice, then, they need to be involved with politics."[2]

Of all people on the planet, one would think we who claim to pattern our lives after the One who "for our sakes became poor" would be some of the most lavishly generous. It is hard to understand that supposed followers of such a servant Savior could arrive at the conclusion that accumulating wealth primarily for one's own sake could be remotely biblical. It's certainly no sin to be wealthy, but as Craig Greenfield says, "Though Jesus never rails against those with six-figure incomes, it seems obvious that he would be resolutely against a six-figure lifestyle in a world where children are starving."[3]

"Do not store up for yourselves treasures on earth," says Jesus (Matt 6:19). Mercy uses money as a tool, for the benefit of others. Storing it up is one thing, but doing it "for yourselves" is the thing Jesus seems to find objectionable. Those containing even a modicum of mercy treat their wealth as a centrifuge that flings needed resources out to those with the greatest need. Kingdom economics is less about *accumulation* and more about *dispersion*.

Generosity doesn't end with giving our tithe, handing a buck to a homeless guy, or with contributing to our church's benevolence fund.

2. Wehner, *Death of Politics*, 7.
3. Greenfield, *Subversive Jesus*, 113.

PART TWO | UTTERLY UPSIDE-DOWN ATTITUDES

Those are good places to begin, but the mercy-filled person cares enough to address the systemic inequitable distribution of opportunity in our culture.

One good example of this is a collaboration of likeminded churches that steward resources in an effort each year to make Christmas a world-changing event again. During the holiday season, when Mammon is on its most frenetic recruiting mission, some justice-conscious churches began the "Advent Conspiracy"[4] based on four primary initiatives: *Worship Fully, Spend Less, Give More, and Love All.* Simply stated: *Put Jesus first and be generous with those who need it most.* This collection of hundreds of churches that are leaning into justice and mercy offer creative alternatives both at home and abroad to the typical consumer-based Mammon-worshipping Christmas holiday season. Check them out.

When we see wealth syphoned away from those who need it most by unjust systems, in order to make a sustainable difference we must pair our merciful attitude with justice-filled action. It's one thing to stand downstream and pull drowning persons out of the river, and another thing to go upstream to prevent them from being shoved in the water to begin with. NGOs like *International Justice Mission*[5] that undertake the rescue and restoration of victims of injustice and the strengthening of justice systems around the world are vital to the church's work of mercy. Check them out.

Systemic injustice is a social, economic, and political reality that excludes and marginalizes people on the basis of race, class, gender, or culture. Mercy pushes against that reality and seeks to replace it with divine justice, aka *shalom*.

> What if our system that drives wages down and prices up in order to maximize profits for billionaire CEOs were infused with a potent dose of mercy-filled Kingdom economics?
>
> What if the assumed privilege of one ethnicity, gender, or class over the other came to terms with the neighbor-loving ways of Jesus?
>
> What if in our quest to be like the Lord we began loving what he loves? "For the LORD is righteous, *he loves justice.*" (Ps 11:7)

---

4. See https://adventconspiracy.org/.
5. See https://www.ijm.org/.

Justice, Mercy's Sibling

Another word from the Bard:

> [Mercy] is an attribute to God himself;
>
> And earthly power doth then show likest God's
>
> When mercy seasons justice.[6]

---

6. From *The Merchant of Venice*, 4.1

Mercy As a Verb

Go and learn what this means: "I desire mercy . . ."
—Matt 9:13

When Jesus came into town, hurting, helpless, hopeless people cried out, "Have mercy on me!"[1] Translation: "Mercy me!" which is to be distinguished from the exclamation equivalent of "Wow" or "Oh my gosh!" Their cry meant, "Please, dump some mercy on me! I don't deserve it, but please, Lord, do for me what I can't do for myself!"

When the blind man called out, "Son of David, have mercy on me!" he wasn't asking for forgiveness or for Jesus to take it easy on him on judgment day. Certainly, he needed those things as well, but his prayer for mercy was about getting his sight back.

Mercy is an action, a verb.

Theologian Walter Brueggemann paraphrases this Beatitude: "Blessed are those who reach out to others with compassion and relieve their needs." Mercy is both an *attitude* and an *action*. If it doesn't lead to some form of action, the attitude is flawed, deficient, or absent.

When Jesus asked which man acted most like a "neighbor" to the half-dead man on the side of the Jericho Road, they said it was the one who "had mercy on him." The Samaritan cleaned the man's wounds, draped him over his donkey, brought him to town, and paid for his ongoing care. That's what mercy looks like. Jesus then said to his audience, "Go and *do* likewise,"[2] not just "Go and *feel* likewise!"

1. Matt 9:27; 15:22; 17:15; 20:30.
2. Luke 10:36–37.

Furthermore, he gave us a clue that mercy entails radical solidarity with and material assistance to the outsider in the name of the God of mercy when he equated "the one who had mercy" with the Samaritan "neighbor" in that same rich parable.

Unfortunately, I can be as calloused as anyone about the suffering of others. I admit, along with Anne Lamott that "On a bad day, I'm pushing old ladies on the Titanic out of the way to get to the lifeboats. (They're old, they're going to die anyway.)" So, I need Jesus to live in and through me especially on my *bad days* and to replenish my stash of mercy to overflowing.

While it's true that doing mercy often includes an emotional reaction to the suffering of others, it goes beyond feeling to doing. Jesus' compassion moved him to take action[3]—to come to earth, to heal the sick, to pass on his wisdom, to sacrifice himself, to rise from the dead, and to empower us to act.

The operative phrase is he "came to earth." He was and is the God who came to be "with us" (Immanuel), who "moved into the neighborhood."[4] "It is not enough (then) to practice charity from a distance," says Eklund. "True mercy, the mercy of the Beatitudes, has to draw close enough to see suffering, to weep with those who weep."[5]

Regarding his impression of Christianity, a state official in India once said: "I had to inspect a plague-stricken town. The inhabitants, frightened, had fled to the fields. The village was deserted, except I saw a missionary lady come down the steps with her hands extended. She came up to my car and said, 'I'm sorry I can't shake hands with you, for my hands are plague-infected.' When I saw those plague-stained hands, then I saw the meaning of the Christian faith."[6]

Empathy, a partial synonym for mercy, is the opposite of *apathy*. Technically, apathy does not mean that we don't care, but that we don't *feel*. "The worst sin towards our fellow creatures is not to hate them," said George Bernard Shaw, "but to be indifferent to them." Mercy, on the other hand, is someone else's pain in my heart, which moves me to do what I can to alleviate their suffering. "Mercy is the ability to get right inside the other person's

---

3. Matt 14:14.
4. John 1:14, The Message Version.
5. Eklund, *Beatitudes through the Ages*, 281.
6. Jones, *Song of Ascents*, 116.

skin until we can see things with his eyes, think things with his mind, and feel things with his feelings."[7]

Thoughts and prayers are always a good place to start. In reference to the suffering of others, we must always pray. But prayer is not always enough. Any dichotomy between prayer and action is a false one. Pray before, during, and after acting—lest your activity be in vain.

No doubt the victims of tragic circumstances appreciate "thoughts and prayers." But if there's something that can be done to alleviate their suffering or overcome an injustice, and it's within our power to do it, I imagine they would appreciate that even more!

Poverty exists not because God does not care but because *we* do not. It exists because we continually edit out large chunks of the divine story that we don't want to hear. The merciful do no such editing.

Christians of good conscience have always lent their hand to those in the most need. You're more likely to find hospitals and orphanages named after saints (St. Luke's, St. Jude's) than ones after even the most famous atheists or agnostics. Can you imagine a *Christopher Hitchens Hospital* or *Bertrand Russell Home for Children*?

Every week a Korean Church in San Francisco brings hamburgers and coffee to people experiencing homelessness. Throughout the winter they give out gloves and scarves, and every year before Christmas they distribute hundreds of expensive jackets. If they don't have your size, they'll go out and buy one. In fact, they bought a bus to pick up homeless people and bring them to their church Bible study. Afterward they bring them to their homes to feed them or buy them a meal in a restaurant. A homeless friend of mine, an atheist (to date), said to me, "These people are the nicest people I've ever met! A fascinating group of people to be around."

Blessed are the merciful!

The early church under Roman rule practiced the politics of mercy by taking home Roman babies who were left to die on the street, especially baby girls who were considered economic liabilities. Though poor in their own right, many Christians acted on the impulse of mercy to adopt the children of their enemies and raise them as their own!

One wonders what would have happened had the church been as apt to serve people afflicted with AIDS in the 1980s as they were to pronounce God's judgment on them. By and large it was a missed opportunity to demonstrate mercy. I was pastoring during those years and admittedly I

---

7. Barclay, *The Beatitudes*, 65.

did nothing to help them personally or to mobilize our church to serve as Jesus would have. I regret my apathy during that time.

Five thousand people a day died at the height of the plagues in the Roman Empire during the second and third centuries. Many people, especially the wealthy, fled from the cities while Christian practitioners stayed to care for the sick. Many of them died as a result of their Christlike service. Some estimate that what they did may have cut the mortality rate during the plague by two thirds!

That's mercy.

Allow me one more line from Portia's appeal to Shylock:

We do pray for mercy;

And that same prayer doth teach us all to render

The deeds of mercy.[8]

---

8. From *The Merchant of Venice*, 4.1

The Merciful and their Money

(The Economics of Jesus)

Where your treasure is, there your heart will be also.
—MATT 6:21

There remains an experience of incomparable value . . . to see the great events of world history from below; from the perspective of the outcast, the suspects, the maltreated, the powerless, the oppressed, the reviled —in short, from the perspective of those who suffer.
—DIETRICH BONHOEFFER[1]

THE ORGANIZATION THAT BUILDS affordable housing for those in need and charges no interest on its mortgage loans, called *Habitat for Humanity*, refers to the core value of their work as "The Economics of Jesus." Nowhere in all his teaching will we find a more concentrated cache of his economic theory than in the Sermon on the Mount.

Smack in the middle of it he delivers a trainload of warning about the "ism" of materialism:

> When you give to the needy. . . . No one can serve two masters. . . . You cannot serve both God and money. . . . Do not worry,

---

1. Bonhoeffer, *Letters and Papers from Prison*, 103.

saying, "What shall we eat?" or "What shall we drink?" or "What shall we wear?" (Matt 6:1, 24–30)

To every money-craving culture he commands us neither to *worship* money (Matt 6:19-24) nor to *worry* about it (Matt 6:25–34). Those who live *beatitudinally*—the mercy-full in particular—refuse to play by this world's rules of engagement or serve its idols. These are the people who choose to love people and use money rather than love money and use people.

In Jesus' *School For Disciples*, the course on money is not an elective. It dominates one of the largest portions of the Sermon, not to mention much of the red letters throughout the Gospels. The class description might read something like: "You can serve God *with money*, but you cannot serve him *and money*."

The merciful know that material things won't fill the hole in their soul. They're so crammed full of mercy that they can't hardly help but give some of it—sometimes a lot of it—away.

The dictum that says you *are more if you have more* couldn't be more contrary to the economics of Jesus. Money is not a goal but a *tool* for the glory of God and the good of people. The merciful are less apt to think in terms of *possessing anything* and more likely to think in terms of *stewarding everything* that God put in their care.

As he challenges the worldview rooted in a lust for *more*, the way he talks about money is subversive, if not downright *intrusive*. How dare he tell us what to do with what's ours—as if anything were actually ours to begin with!

Heaven's social order intended for earth involves an upside-down perspective on money and all it acquires. Though US legal tender asserts, "In God We Trust," you'd never know it by the way we chase after it, hoard it, and waste it.

Jesus says that earthly treasures are fragile and fleeting, subject to rats, bugs, and burglars (Matt 6:19). If he were to visit America today, he might have to put it another way:

> Lay not up for yourselves treasures upon the earth, where falling markets and depreciating bonds doth consume, and where unethical hedge fund managers and unprincipled politicians break through and steal.

Jesus' generation experienced as much disparity between rich and poor as we have in ours. The filthy rich and the bone-grinding poor shared the same air but not nearly the same opportunities. Rome's Jewish puppet-priests and other collaborators had the economy sewn up, leaving any chance for economic advance only to those who were willing to play along, defy God, and betray their countrymen.

While Jesus doesn't lay down specific monetary policies or order all of us to live at or below a certain net worth, he does provide a moral framework for our economic decisions. He invites us to buy into his kingdom economic theory and compels us to live free of Mammon's tentacles. The key, he says, is in what we treasure. "Do not treasure your earthly treasures,"[2] for some things simply don't deserve to be treasured.

"The place where your treasure is, is the place you will most want to be, and end up being."[3] If we want to end up in a better place than earthly riches can take us, we have to treasure that which is worthy of being treasured. Our inventions and "pretty toys," wrote Thoreau, "are but improved means to an unimproved end."[4]

What some people would consider *necessities*, others would think of as *luxuries*. Excess is the new normal. This is why the founder of the Catholic Worker Movement, Dorothy Day, used to say, "We must talk about poverty, because people insulated by their own comfort lose sight of it."

Many Christians—rich or poor—tend to interpret Jesus' economic values through the lens of their preferred material lifestyle. Their bank accounts come first while their values follow conveniently behind like well-trained pets. Jesus, on the other hand, demands that we make our economic decisions under his tutelage.

Since the 1950s the average size of an American house has nearly tripled, while family size has decreased by 30 percent. Many are now finding that *more is less* and the exponential *biggering* of their property and possessions has not necessarily improved their quality of life. What good is a bigger house, car, or portfolio if our walk with God and our witness to the world has shrunk?

Some calculate that the United States ranks around the 30th percentile in global income inequality, which means that 70 percent of the world's countries have a more equitable income distribution than ours. Even more culpable, in my opinion, is our yearly expenditure of $10 billion on church buildings and the cumulative value of the church's real estate at over $230

---

2. The best translation of Matt 6:19.
3. The Message paraphrase of Matt 6:21.
4. Thoreau, *Walden*, 149.

billion. Someone said that God uses the cries of those who suffer in poverty to call the church out of its soundproof sanctuaries! May we hear their call and practice mercy.

We weren't made to consume more than we need. We know this because when we gorge ourselves, even on healthy food, our stomachs scream, "Get thee to the Pepto!" Rather than stockpiling their surplus, people who are full of mercy share their bounty with those who have less. When Mammon tempts them to do otherwise they pray David's prayer:

> Give me an appetite for your words of wisdom, and not for piling up loot. Divert my eyes from toys and trinkets, invigorate me on the pilgrim way. (Ps 119:36–37, The Message Bible)

Mammon Worship

No one can serve two masters. Either you will hate the one and love the other, or you will be devoted to the one and despise the other. You cannot serve both God and money.

—Matt 6:24

We have endowed money with our own psychic energy giving it arms and legs... We enshrine it in a secret place, give it a heart and mind and the power to grant us peace and mercy.

—Elizabeth O'Connor

"Mammon" is the Aramaic term for money that Luke preserved in his version of Jesus' parallel teaching in Luke 16. He probably chose it to denote the false-god status that money often plays in our lives—like Baal, Zeus, or the idol called *The American Dream*. Mammon represents how we've turned wealth into a living thing by trusting it to protect us, make us happy, or give us power.

Greed is an idol (Eph 5:5 and Col 3:5), and as with any false deity, material things have no spiritual power aside from what we ascribe to them by making them objects of our worship. Mammon requires the kind of allegiance, love, and service that must be reserved only for God. It promises anything, demands everything, and delivers nothing.

Sadly, a sizeable chunk of Western Christians, whose god measures its devotees' worth through their investment portfolios, have as their mantra: *In the Market We Trust!* They've *bought into* the spirit of the age and conduct themselves no differently from those whose messiah is the *Lord Dollar Almighty*.

Think of how the cavernous gap between rich and poor would be narrowed if everyone sought just enough to meet their immediate needs and shared the rest with those who are in greater need! Enough should be enough, especially when there are so many in the world who never experience enough. John Wesley asked how is the command to "Lay not up treasures for yourselves on earth" any different than "Thou shalt not commit adultery"? (They're both commands. Right?) Wesley went on to say, "How then can any man who has already the necessaries of life, gain or aim at more, and be guiltless?"

One of Jesus' first followers abandoned him for money. He claimed to care about the poor but was a thief of the worst sort, the sort that robs the offering plate!

The fervor to fix our broken selves by accumulating stuff is an errand only fools sign up for. Anne Lamott compares it to shopping for bread at the hardware store. "It doesn't sell bread."[1]

Mammon worship is *not* a victimless crime. Loving money is at the "root of many kinds of evil,"[2] including the evil it does to the fabric of any society. The negative social implications of "American Affluenza" are countless. Overconsumption not only infects one's own soul with stress and one's body with ulcers, it breeds rot in the culture by increasing pitiless rivalries and economic disparity, not to mention environmental damage.

Jesus didn't say that we *should not* serve two masters, but that we *cannot*. It's a law as inexorable as gravity. We can't very well hoard our wealth and hold onto Jesus at the same time. The effort to oblige conflicting loyalties is a lose-lose proposition. In trying to please one, we end up displeasing the other. If we strain to serve both God and Mammon we'll most likely end up denying God and deferring to Mammon. "Our hearts have room only for one all-embracing devotion, and we can only cleave to one Lord."[3]

Richard Rohr says that as a Catholic priest he's heard thousands of confessions over the years, yet he's never heard even one about violating the Tenth Commandment, the one about coveting our neighbor's possessions!

---

1. Lamott, *Almost Everything*, 35.
2. 1 Tim 6:10.
3. Bonhoeffer, *Cost of Discipleship*, 59.

Part Two | Utterly Upside-Down Attitudes

"Since Mammon is a particularly unruly type of god when it's anywhere except on the throne, it will be necessary in some instances to put it completely *outside* in order to keep it quiet."[4] Mammon's kingdom is best described by dehumanizing poverty and dehumanizing consumerism. We must learn to put it outside and out of our misery by starving it with generosity.

---

4. Jordan, *Sermon on the Mount*, 73.

Mammon's Predatory Preachers

Watch out for false prophets . . . by their fruit you will recognize them.
—MATT 7:15, 20

WHEN ASKED WHETHER OR not God promises riches for his followers, the great Billy Graham said: "Jesus wasn't rich, nor were His first disciples. In fact, the only disciple who really cared about money was Judas, whose greed and unbelief caused him to betray Jesus for 30 pieces of silver."[1]

This world is not our oyster, or the earth our personal cash cow, the mix of metaphors—mollusks and bovine—notwithstanding. The blessed task of the merciful is to contribute to the most vulnerable, "take care" of the garden God gave us, and steward its resources under his tutelage for the common good.

In order to make his point about the kingdom way of relating to wealth, Jesus made a passing reference to the Bible's biggest Mammonite, whose misdirected ambition for more and more wealth and fame is legendary: "Not even Solomon in all his splendor was dressed like one of these [flowers of the field]" (Matt 6:29). David's favored son shamelessly took nearly a thousand wives and amassed a mountain of gold and silver, not to mention a warehouse full of the latest clothing fashions. The flowers bloom by God's design and are clothed more beautifully than even Israel's most affluent monarch, so trust him to put clothes on your back and don't be so impressed with the Solomons of this world.

Predatory preachers throughout church history have modeled their ministries more after Solomon than Jesus. These "experts in greed . . . seduce

---

1. Graham, "Does God Want Everyone," para. 2.

the unstable" for their own profit.² Out of one side of their mouth they complain about the evils of the world and from the other side they demand its riches and resources as their rightful inheritance. They preach that God includes in our salvation package a no-limit gift card to consume as much as we can without any regard to what is best for our neighbors.

Jesus was no stranger to the Mammonites of his own time. Like any number of self-indulgent prosperity preachers of our day, his contemporaries, the Jerusalem-based aristocratic priesthood, flaunted their wealth, which they syphoned off poor and trusting souls.

The kind of prosperity that we clamor for in this life will mean zilch in the next. Most of what we treasure here feeds the moths or rusts away to nothing (Matt 6:19–20). In the next world we'll be so enamored with our eternal treasures that the things that we deemed so central here will, by comparison, be cheap costume jewelry.

The "prosperity gospel" (which bears little resemblance to the gospel of Jesus Christ) and its Mammon-worshiping "evangelists" with their $10,000 suits, personal jets, and multiple mansions, promise health and wealth on demand for everyone who possesses enough of their brand of faith. They confuse material prosperity with Christianity, yet in God's inverted kingdom it's mercy that measures our humanity and compassion that explains our Christianity.

They may prophesy, send demons back to hell, and walk on water in his name yet they do everything except what God actually commands them to do. They may be orthodox in their theology and lead grandiose organizations but lacking meekness, mercy, and purity of heart, they do any old thing they want when they want to (Matt 7:21–23).

Mammon-glazed preachers require Mammon-seeking followers, consumer Christians, whose salt has long since washed away and whose light is obscured by their lust for more and more money and power. They've forgotten that we're here as *ambassadors* not as consumers.

Jesus makes clear that to be materially prosperous isn't the same as being morally virtuous. The Roman Empire, for example, was powerful and prosperous yet could hardly have been considered *virtuous*. If we sacrifice moral goodness on the altar of material gain for a select few at the top of the socioeconomic food chain, we doom ourselves to the same fate as any number of ancient civilizations, not to mention defunct historic denominations.

2. 2 Pet 2:14.

Mammon's Predatory Preachers

The "prosperity" promised by devious preachers and politicians can't begin to rival the blessedness that Jesus bestows on beatitude-practicing believers. The poor in spirit possess the kingdom, mourners are comforted, the meek inherit the earth, those who hunger for justice are filled, and the merciful overflow with mercy!

Money Worries Mute Mercy

Do not worry, saying, "What shall we eat?" or "What shall we drink?" or "What shall we wear?" For the pagans run after all these things, and your heavenly Father knows that you need them. But seek first his kingdom and his righteousness, and all these things will be given to you as well. Therefore do not worry about tomorrow, for tomorrow will worry about itself. Each day has enough trouble of its own.

—Matt 6:31–34

Earthly possessions dazzle our eyes and delude us into thinking that they can provide security and freedom from anxiety. Yet all the time they are the very source of all anxiety.

—Dietrich Bonhoeffer[1]

If Mammon can't entice us to worship it, it will tempt us to live in constant *worry about it*. In some ways the results are the same, a watered-down faith and an anxious mind.

Jesus didn't say these things in a vacuum. His audiences were predominantly made up of very low-income to no-income Jews, who, due to oppressive taxation and debt bondage, had zero opportunity to pull themselves up by their sandal straps.

As a fairly educated white American male, when I'm financially strapped it's because I'm forced to pay only the minimum payment on my credit card bill or have no actual paper money in my entertainment

---

1. Bonhoeffer, *Cost of Discipleship*, 80.

envelope for the month. My financial state may be meager by American Dream standards, but it could hardly be considered *dire.*

For most Americans, the question, "What shall we eat?" (Matt 6:31) usually refers to choosing between steak with potatoes and chicken with rice. "What shall we drink?" means nothing more stressful than the choice between white wine, red wine, or Perrier. And the predicament they face while staring forlornly at a closet crammed with clothes, asking themselves, "What shall we wear?" has to do with the terribly tough decision between sport coat or no coat, dress or designer jeans.

The things we often fret about don't even show up on the radar of most of the world's inhabitants. They're praying for "daily bread" not deciding whether to pay with cash or plastic for the $100-per-person dinner at their favorite restaurant.

Anxiety over money not only disturbs our spirituality and blood pressure, it also impairs our social conscience. It seems the socioeconomic well-being of those in greatest need is way down the list for most voters while choosing candidates that promise to improve their own bottom line at the expense of the common good. It doesn't even occur to many Americans to support candidates and vote for initiatives that advantage the disadvantaged even at the disadvantage of the over-advantaged.

We can't very well be *full of worry* and *full of mercy* at the same time. Worry is a notorious mercy thief. Fretting over money reduces our mercy reserves and hinders our hunger for justice for all. It burrows into our hearts and saps our compassion. As we "run after" money we're likely to sprint right past mercy.

That said, most of us still worry about money to one degree or another. When Jesus urged his congregation sitting on the grass that day not to worry, he wanted to spare them (and us) from the adverse effects that worry has on our souls, not to mention on our bodies and our relationships.

> Give your entire attention to what God is doing right now, and don't get worked up about what may or may not happen tomorrow. God will help you deal with whatever hard things come up when the time comes. (Matt 6:34, The Message)

Mercy Starves Mammon

Give to the one who asks you, and do not turn away from the one who wants to borrow from you.

—MATT 5:42

The test of our progress is not whether we add more to the abundance of those who have much; it is whether we provide enough for those who have too little.

—FRANKLIN D. ROOSEVELT

MAMMON IS A MONSTER always famished. Feeding it fortifies it and starving it weakens it, if not places it on life support. Wherever its absence is greater than its presence we starve it by seeking God's just kingdom. To mercy-filled followers, few things require more attention than liberty and justice *for all*. They care particularly about people who have been shoved to the margins and whose appeals for justice go largely unheeded.

Unfortunately, this is less than descriptive of the priorities of much of Western Church culture. If we're being honest with ourselves, we would have to admit that we spend more time seeking our own right to bigger houses, faster cars, and chicer wardrobes than seeking justice for the disadvantaged.

Radical simplicity and reckless generosity are mercy's two favorite techniques of starving Mammon and spreading justice. In our culture of excess, we best tame the *more monster* by learning to live with less and giving away more.

Simplicity

> Simplicity sets us free to receive the provision of God as a gift that is not ours to keep and can be freely shared with others.[1]

There's no mistaking that Jesus lived simply and invited us join him into the same with his word pictures: *the birds of the air, the flowers of the meadows, and the grass of the fields* (Matt 6:26, 28, 30). Entirely foreign to him was the daily stress of acquiring and accumulating. The same is true for those who find rest for their souls by choosing his easy yoke.[2]

I once visited the apartment of a genuine hoarder and can attest to the wisdom of Jesus' warning that heaping up stuff may well attract *bugs and vermin* (Matt 6:19). "Kathryn" had only one piece of furniture left (a small slice of her single bed) that wasn't piled chin high with used newspapers, food wrappers, and boxes filled with who knows what. Instantly I felt invaded by fleas and probably other things I'd rather not think about. As soon as politely possible I made for the door, drove home like a madman, showered three times, and drenched myself in an industrial anti-every-kind-of-bug-known-to-man solution. Years later I still itch when I think about it!

Her house was the antithesis of *simplicity*. She had asked me to help her clean up her place but as she was unwilling to part with any of her "treasures" my efforts were more frustrating than fruitful. Makes me wonder if the Lord feels similarly when he attempts to wrest our *treasures* from our iron grip. While we might not treasure what she treasures or succumb to a classic case of hoarders' disease, we're all vulnerable to some strain of the virus. But whatever you chase after and stockpile for yourself your heart will sheepishly follow to the ends of the earth (Matt 6:21).

You may not fill your house with trash but if you make a "searching and fearless moral inventory"[3] of your heart and home, you might discover an addiction to certain preferred possessions of yours. Those obsessed with material things deplete their resources and damage their testimony, while those whose focus and budget reflects radical contentment are free to show mercy to the neediest of their neighbors near and far.

---

1. Foster, *Celebration of Discipline*, 85.
2. Matt 11:30.
3. Step four of AA's Twelve-Step program.

Part Two | Utterly Upside-Down Attitudes

Simplicity is a daily choice to leverage our time, treasure, and talents toward what matters most.[4] "There are two ways to get enough," wrote G. K. Chesterton. "One is to continue to accumulate more and more. The other is to desire less."

Desiring less is something Solomon, who clothed himself "in splendor" (Matt 6:29), might have done well to consider. Being content with a smaller and simpler wardrobe, to say nothing of taking on fewer wives, would have greatly improved his life and legacy. An old Amish mantra says, "To desire to be rich is to desire to have more than what we need to be content."

Overconsumption injures our relationship with the Creator, does untold damage to his creation, and reduces our storehouse of mercy for those in need. The practice of simplicity reduces our global footprint, paves the way for a more sustainable lifestyle for future generations, and adds to the credibility of our message. "What's good for the soul is good for the pocketbook and also for the planet."[5]

Is it a sin to live in a 10,000 square foot house or drive a car that will go twice as fast as the speed limit (in reverse!), or own an article of clothing worth more than most people's yearly mortgage payment? Maybe we should reframe the question:

>Do I need this thing or just want it?
>
>If I own it, how likely is it that it will eventually own me?
>
>Would it serve a purpose or just massage my ego?
>
>While I may be able to afford it, in a world with such dire need, can others afford for me to waste my money on a status symbol?

Make no mistake, *simpler* is not the same as *easier*. True simplicity is actually harder as it runs against the grain of a decidedly Mammon worshipping materialistic culture. But long-range kingdom gains of simplifying in order to unleash compassion and unmute mercy, more than make the effort worthwhile.[6]

---

4. Scandrette, *Free*, 91.
5. Scandrette, *Free*, 53.
6. Here is some suggested reading on the topic of simplicity:
Simple Spirituality: Learning to See God in a Broken World by Christopher Heuertz
Free: Spending Your Time And Money On What Matters Most by Mark Scandrette
Simpler Living, Compassionate Life, edited and compiled by Michael Schut
The Freedom of Simplicity by Richard Foster
The Shakertown Pledge, https://en.wikipedia.org/wiki/The_Shakertown_Pledge

Generosity

> Mammon cannot tolerate generosity. Generosity undermines the very foundation it is built upon. By using our wealth in the faithful way Jesus has described, we exorcize the demonic force bound up with Mammon, and it becomes an instrument of the kingdom of God.[7]

Shamelessly merciful people living in simplicity are nearly incapable of being indifferent to those less fortunate than them. They live with less in order to give away more. Instead of confusing any bounty that comes their way as entitlement, they interpret it as an opportunity to act generously.

Between his "treasures" and "masters" metaphors, Jesus injected a slightly enigmatic Hebrew idiom about eyesight, which his audience would have recognized as a reference to greed versus generosity.

> The eye is the lamp of the body. If your eyes are healthy, your whole body will be full of light. But if your eyes are unhealthy, your whole body will be full of darkness. If then the light within you is darkness, how great is that darkness! (Matt 6:22–23)

People with good eyes (figuratively speaking) are generous. Unlike their nearsighted, tightfisted counterparts, who can't see past the wart on their nose, the generous are able to see *beyond themselves*. Stingy people aren't capable of seeing what God sees, for needy people live beyond their line of sight. Those who see with God's eyes, like him, are willing to freely share themselves and their possessions.

"How great is the darkness" in which the greedy person blindly gropes! The generous soul, on the other hand, has "healthy" eyes and a "body full of light." I take this to mean that not only are they able to see where they're going, they're positively radiant! As "the light of the world" they illuminate the way before them so that others can walk in their light![8]

Mammon's idolatrous business plan runs solely on the promise of personal profit and takes no account for the common good. As long as keeping a slave or raping the planet improves their bottom line, Mammonites feel no compunction about how they make or spend their

---

7. Engdahl, *Great Chasm*, 61.

8. The Message Bible's paraphrase captures Jesus' meaning quite well I think: "Your eyes are windows into your body. If you open your eyes wide in wonder and belief, your body fills up with light. If you live squinty-eyed in greed and distrust, your body is a musty cellar. If you pull the blinds on your windows, what a dark life you will have!"

money. Their relationships are purely utilitarian, as they care nothing for anyone who is unable to benefit them. In contrast to the merciful, they care nothing for the aged, the sick, widows, orphans, or strangers.

"Anyone who has two shirts should share with the one who has none," said John the Baptizer, "and anyone who has food should do the same."[9] I know a church in San Francisco that did an experiment based on this passage called "Have Two, Give One." In order to live out what they call "radical generosity" they decided to sell or giveaway any of their duplicate possessions and donate the proceeds to global poverty relief. "Our goal wasn't to be exacting or legalistic," says Pastor Mark Scandrette, "but to playfully engage each other to live more freely and generously."[10]

For the following eight weeks each person in the group chose a category of possessions to sell, share, or giveaway. One week it would be clothes, another week, books and music, and another week, larger household items like cars and bicycles. Sometimes they gave these items to someone else in the church that needed them more. Other times they sold and donated the money to a charity of their choice. "It was shocking to find out how little some of our possessions were worth and disappointing that we regarded them as so precious."[11]

I heard of another example of radical generosity where a young mother sent a package containing a handful of used baby pacifiers to the *Word Made Flesh Ministry*.[12] The accompanying letter said:

> Our two-year-old daughter Grace and I have a little prayer book that we pray through each night. Grace has been adamant about sending her "bobbie's" to poor children. She has even picked out which children will receive which colors that will make them "feel all better." Even though she no longer uses her pacifiers, she is attached to them as she remembers that they always made her feel better. They are really precious to her. Please accept these on behalf of the children you encounter and know that there is a two-year-old in Alabama who sincerely loves and prays for them.

Jesus' advice to those whose net income doesn't support their gross lifestyle would be to keep their *wanting* low and engender a joyful unconcern for possessions so that they have more to share with others.

9. Luke 3:11.
10. Scandrette, *Free*, 133.
11. Scandrette, *Free*, 133.
12. See https://wordmadeflesh.org/.

Mercy Starves Mammon

Like fish out of water, Mammon cannot survive in an atmosphere of generosity. When we share some of our hard-earned money with those who need it more than we do, we suffocate our craving for money and repurpose it as an instrument for the kingdom of God.

God demands our idols. At least on one occasion Jesus required a man to sell everything and give the proceeds to the poor. Sadly, the man preferred his temporary wealth to eternal life. It appears he expected salvation to be a little less costly and a little more comfy. Like so many in the modern world he was securely berthed in his wealth from which Jesus called him to unmoor in order to navigate out into the open sea of eternal adventure.

As God's unqualified love gradually recalibrates our means of achieving self-worth, our need to possess our possessions with such ferocity dissipates. Our social capital and the influence it wields shifts from earthly success to the advance of the culture of heaven.

In the twenty years since Bill and Melinda Gates created their foundation, they have invested $53.8 billion on global health and development. They say they're "still swinging for the fences," which is advice Warren Buffett, another extravagantly generous philanthropist, gave them years ago. Their main concern now is that innovation be distributed equitably. "If only some people in some places are benefitting from new advances, then others are falling even further behind. . . . We believe that progress should benefit everyone, everywhere."[13]

That's what I call healthy eyes and a body full of light![14]

Shakespeare had it right about mercy. It is not something forced (i.e., strain'd) but falls like a gentle rain from heaven. And when it does, both the benefactor and the beneficiary are blessed together.[15]

---

13. Gates and Gates, "Why We Swing for the Fences," para. 125.

14. Here are some faith-based organizations that focus on addressing world hunger:
World Vision: https://www.worldvision.org
Bread for the World: https://www.bread.org/
Food for the Hungry: https://www.fh.org/about/
World Hunger Relief: http://www.worldhungerrelief.org/
Samaritan's Purse: https://www.samaritanspurse.org/

15. Often called "the American Mother Teresa," Dorothy Day would be on my short list of remarkable examples of mercy. As a result of her work with the poor she has also been called "the saint for difficult people." She used to say, "Those who cannot see Christ

The Uncluttered Heart

Blessed are the pure in heart for they shall see God.
—Matt 5:8

Great beauty, great strength, and great riches are really and truly of no great use; a right heart exceeds all.
—Benjamin Franklin

As we've seen, Jesus' Manifesto is the ultimate counternarrative to the story the world tells itself. It provides an alternative worldview. *Pure hearts* deserve a place on the short list of kingdom characteristics particularly counterintuitive to our convoluted culture. It's rare to find a person whose heart contains little to no clutter. Let's just round that "rare" down to none.

Earlier I referred to my visit to the home of a hoarder where empty cereal boxes, old newspapers, and the like were piled so high you could hardly see from one room to the next. The paths she left in order to negotiate between them were like a garden labyrinth in which the walls between passages are crafted of tall hedges. You could only see what the clutter permitted you to see.

God didn't plant the hedges or create the mess to keep us guessing where he is and what he's up to. We're the ones responsible for the clutter in our hearts, which obstructs our view of him and his activities.

Those with a pure heart are no stranger to the first five blessed attitudes, which have a decluttering influence on one's inner life. Acknowledging

---

in the poor are atheists indeed." For more on her exemplary life, read *Loaves and Fishes: The Inspiring Story of the Catholic Worker Movement.*

spiritual poverty, grieving it, being humbled by it, hungering to improve it, and becoming acquainted with mercy as a result of it, clear a path through the clutter inside.

The pure-hearted can "see God" because their sight isn't impaired by trying to focus on more than one thing at the same time. The outlook of *cross-eyed Christians* is blurred by competing concerns. The only thing worse than spiritual blindness is thinking you can see when you can't.[1] Viewing God through spiritual cataracts is at best, limiting, and at worst, ruinous.

The chapters ahead will highlight how the uncluttered heart leads to an unimpeded view of what matters. It affects our gender ethics (Matt 5:27–28, 31–32), transforms our practice of the spiritual disciplines (Matt 6:1–5), improves our vision of his activities (John 5:19), and invites us to raise our voice with his for the sake of the voiceless (Prov 31:8).

---

1. Rev 3:18.

Healthy on the Inside

Jesus points us to an inner innocence and childlike wonder that keeps us open to the presence of God. With that inner innocence, we begin to see God around us.

—JOHN DEAR[1]

THE PATIENT MAY LOOK perfectly well on the outside but when Dr. God places his stethoscope on their chest, what will he hear? Religious experts take great pains to clean the outside of cups and decorate tombs but Jesus calls our attention to their contents.[2]

As we've been saying all along, the entire Sermon reflects an inside-out vantage point in which Jesus gets *to the heart of the matter*. In order to understand, let alone *obey* everything he teaches, we need to be pure in our inner-self.

If you ask people to identify their most important organ, I suspect most would cite their heart. The importance of this blood-pumping, oxygen-distributing muscle can't be overstated for maintaining one's physical health. The Bible routinely uses the "heart" as a metaphor to describe what's going on inside a person. Like the organ concealed inside our chest, this deeper part of us is visible only to God and delivers life-sustaining help to the rest of our person.

---

1. Dear, *Beatitudes of Peace*, 66.
2. Matt 23:26–28. Inner purity wasn't lost on David either: Ps 24:4; 51:10; 73:1.

We are advised to guard this divine depository because everything we do "flows from it."[3] Good people store up good things in their good hearts and then share them with others.[4]

A pure heart is developed over time. It's not something we *achieve* so much as what we *receive* during the incremental process of learning how to cooperate with the live-in Holy Spirit. He works best with a heart that's supple enough to be kneaded into a shape that closer resembles the image of God.

Phillips translates *pure* as "utterly sincere," that is, without pretense. Pure-hearted folk don't fake it or use their faith to deceive people or manipulate God. They're real.

Years ago one of our church members told me, "Pastor, I love our church, but one thing I love more is my AA group." When I asked why, she said, "We're more honest there." It gave me pause to think that maybe if we had a little less pomposity and a little more sincerity, we'd reach more people thirsting for the authentic.

Jesus had no divisions, no dueling motives or hidden agendas. Paul juxtaposes the pure heart with "a good conscience and a sincere faith" (1 Tim 1:5). Those whose inner person is uncluttered are less driven by duplicitous motives. They don't finagle faith into self-promotion, but above all else they are single-mindedly determined to make God happy.

Rest assured, a pure heart doesn't imply a heart free from all imperfections, but one that relentlessly pursues the pure heart of God. Purity has more to do with *sincerity* than sinlessness and is more about the heart's *direction* than its perfection. It's more of an acknowledgement of our frailty plus an unreserved confidence in God to make us stronger disciples.

We live in the tension between a humble recognition of our imperfections (*poor in spirit*) and a sincere devotion to innocence (*pure in heart*). Our heart becomes purer by the collaborative effort between the Holy Spirit and our spirit.

The essence of a "pure heart" is its pure love for its Maker and all he's made. It was created to circulate love for God and neighbor throughout the entire human personality. Those whose hearts are permeated with love, offer themselves to others in sacrificial service and work to transform the world to better resemble Jesus' new order.

---

3. Prov 4:23.

4. Luke 6:45.

Jesus on How To Treat Women

You have heard that it was said, 'You shall not commit adultery.' But I tell you that anyone who looks at a woman lustfully has already committed adultery with her in his heart.

—Matt 5:27–28

It has been said, "Anyone who divorces his wife must give her a certificate of divorce." But I tell you that anyone who divorces his wife, except for sexual immorality, makes her the victim of adultery, and anyone who marries a divorced woman commits adultery.

—Matt 5:31–32

Women are made in God's image and are therefore like God. Men are too, but most of us are already convinced of it and don't need any reminders!

If you think that Eve was inferior to Adam because she was made after him, consider this. Usually things made second are an *improvement* on the first. As a writer I know that my second drafts are always much better than my first one. God made Adam, stepped back and thought, "This is really good, but I think I can do better!" So he made a woman. And she was *really, really good!*

He said that Eve would be a "helper suitable" for the man, which has often been misinterpreted to mean she was a second-class human, made just to serve the man. Actually, the phrase implies she was a mirror image of her partner. She's different from him (you probably already knew that) but

Jesus on How To Treat Women

in another sense very much the same as her associate-divine-image bearer, Adam. Eve was no pawn, but a *partner*, not a slave but a *soul mate*.

Let's not forget that Jesus was at the meeting when the agenda item about populating the planet with people was being voted on. The Three agreed: "Let *us* make humans."[1] So, it's no surprise that Jesus, having grown up in a decidedly misogynistic culture, when it was time to launch his ministry, made a point of insisting that men must treat women as equals.

When we think of "purity," for men in particular, sexual integrity most often comes to mind. The detoxifying influence of Jesus' kingship has a profound effect on our sexual ethics, in both personal and social contexts. There are few things more corrosive to the soul than a hedonistic sexual ethic, and nothing more fundamental to the health of the social fabric than the relationship between the sexes, particularly the sanctity of the marriage bond. Both of which he addresses in his Sermon, surely to the shock of the men in his audience.

Jesus practiced and preached a radical inversion of male self-indulgent social norms. One would be hard-pressed to identify anything more anti-kingdom than the denigration and exploitation of women in any past or present culture.

The *pure in heart* are highly motivated to row upstream against the cultural current and model the healthy sexual mores of the heavenly kingdom.

Anti-Kingdom Gender Roles

In a culture of unlimited male power and privilege, Jesus' check on male patriarchy is one of his most socially subversive teachings. His association in public with women who were not his kin was a scandalous breech of decorum and a challenge to the gender boundaries of first-century culture.

The Greco-Roman and Hebrew civilizations of Jesus' day acknowledged few if any social or spiritual rights for women. In Roman law it was illegal for a widow to go more than two years without remarrying. She was forced to marry or go hungry.

The dismal status of a woman in Hebrew society was no better, if not worse, as she was crammed into the bottom of the barrel alongside slaves. Her husband could divorce her for talking to another man in public. If he didn't like how his wife looked in the morning he could declare before

---

1. Gen 1:26; John 1:1–3; Col 1:16.

witnesses their marriage was null and void. Just like that, he kicks her to the curb.

Women had no recourse to divorce their husbands for any reason, including their own survival. In most cases the divorced woman would be abandoned and not permitted to remarry. She was shamed and reduced to beggary, prostitution, or some other humiliation for the rest of her life.

After twenty centuries of economic inequality, workplace discrimination, and sexual harassment, not to mention domestic violence and sexual assault, even the church is often content to look the other way. Male entitlement and predatory behavior have no place in a civil world, let alone among the people called "Christian." Sadly, toxic masculinity still exists in some sectors of the church where women are commodified and treated like property.

He Flips the Script

Jesus' positively *pure-hearted* way of relating to women was outright scandalous by comparison to their men-first-and-foremost culture.

In his interaction with the woman at the well he broke all the rules regarding religious, ethnic, and worst of all, gender biases. An argument could be made that it was to her that he first clearly disclosed his identity as Messiah. Later he held a one-on-one Bible study with a female friend who sat at his feet and soaked up everything he taught. (Women had no such personal access to rabbinical teaching.) And after he rose again he chose a group of women to make the announcement of his resurrection to the male apostles, thereby demonstrating a new and radical precedent for gender equality.

He transformed Saul into Paul who declared: "There is neither Jew nor Gentile, neither slave nor free, nor is there male and female, for you are all one in Christ Jesus."[2] The boxes in which the genders had been packaged for centuries were torn open and would no longer hold them. Equality becomes the new normal for those who choose the upside-down way of Jesus.

Male sexual lust and male-initiated divorce, both of which denigrate and damage women, are the two things he confronts in the Manifesto. In these two extraordinary examples of *a pure heart,* he exposes the abuse of male power and gender exploitation, and puts everyone on equal footing.

2. Gal 3:28.

Jesus on How To Treat Women

He teaches men to value women as equals instead of as objects to ogle. He requires husbands to treasure their wives rather than discard them as so much rubbish. In both cases Jesus looks out for the woman and demands that she be treated as a counterpart with dignity and respect. In his new order she is no longer candy for the eye or compost for the trash heap. She's to be honored as unique yet equal.

> If we believe that in Christ "there is no longer male or female," it's time for men to do their part in confronting and teaching their brothers and working in solidarity with their sisters to make this vision of God's love a reality in our churches and in the world.[3]

---

3. Wallis, *Christ in Crisis?*, 65.

Pure-Hearted Practitioners

Be careful not to practice your righteousness in front of others to be seen by them . . . When you give to the needy . . . When you pray . . . When you fast . . .

—Matt 6:1, 2, 3, 5

Disciple: Is there anything I can do to make myself enlightened?
Teacher: As little as you can do to make the sun rise in the morning.
Disciple: Then of what use are the spiritual exercises you prescribe?
Teacher: To make sure you are not asleep when the sun begins to rise.
—Anthony de Mello

Giving, praying, and fasting don't exhaust the list of biblical spiritual practices. Jesus singles these out as samples of how a pure-hearted person practices his or her faith for the right reasons. He speaks to our inclination to do spiritual stuff for the cheers of our fans like the defensive back dancing his victory jig after intercepting a pass and scoring a touchdown.

Those with a pure heart give, pray, and fast *for the glory of God and the good of people*, while those whose heart contains more pretention than purity do these things for their own glory and good.

In another place Jesus posed the prayer of the pretentious: "God, I thank you that I am not like other people. . . . I fast twice a week and give a tenth of all I get." The man's gratuitous use of "I's" (four in the span of two sentences) betrays his claim to a superior spirituality. In contrast, the self-admitted sinner wouldn't so much as presume to look God in the eye.

Pure-Hearted Practitioners

Instead, he beat his chest and simply pled for mercy (Luke 18:10–14). In spite of his personal failings, that latter man possessed the purer and more honest heart.

While giving, praying, and fasting yield much personal fruit, we must not horde the harvest we glean but deliver it to others. Personal benefits aside, we must see the significant social implications of compassion-filled spiritual practices. The disciplines improve pure-hearted persons, not just for their own personal progress, but so they can facilitate improvement in the world around them.

The question we're asking as we process Jesus' teaching is: *What on earth?* What is the point of us being *in this world* if we're not going to challenge its inherently diseased status quo with the healthy alternative of God's kingdom? Has he not commissioned us to partner with him in his project of moving the cultural needle in the direction of his better-world paradigm? These disciplines (so-called) are designed to make better disciples on earth, not super spiritual people who want to escape it.

Pretentious posers concern themselves with maintaining their image and care little about making the world a better place for their neighbors. When self-congratulating saints do the disciplines, the benefits end with them—they "have their reward in full" (Matt 6:2, 5, 16). Unlike the pure-hearted, their vision of God is opaque. All they see is their own face in the mirror while they primp and preen.

Those who possess pure hearts engage in giving, praying, and fasting in such a way as to reach far beyond themselves in order to fill the vacuum of human need in the world around them.

Single-Minded Seers

You're blessed when you get your inside world—your mind and heart—put right. Then you can see God in the outside world.
—Matt 5:8, The Message

When the heart is right, seeing will be right. All we need do is keep the lens clean. If your heart is cold, your vision is distorted.
—Richard Rohr[1]

Pure-hearted and clear-seeing are symbiotic. The pure in heart see God, and those who see God purify their hearts.

They can see him because their vision is not impaired by idols competing for their attention. Trying to maintain two masters at the same time is inadvisable and, according to Jesus (Matt 6:24), impossible. Focusing on two objects simultaneously blurs them both and makes us cross-eyed, double-minded, and unstable.[2]

While it's true that we only "see a poor reflection [of him] as in a mirror," the purer our hearts, the better the reflection we'll see today until one day we see him "face to face."

That said, "seeing" God is not an end in itself. Because he's active, those who see him in action want to act with him.[3] Of course, in the glorified state we'll see him, but not just so we can stare at him forever. OK, so

---

1. Rohr, *Jesus' Plan for a New World*, 69.
2. Jas 1:8; 4:8.
3. John 5:17.

maybe for the first thousand years or so of the celestial honeymoon period we'll gawk at the Glory. But unless I'm mistaken, he will quickly put us to work as eternal reflections of that Glory.

"Seeing" God in Action

How is it that the pure in heart are able to "see God"? Though people have forever tried to imagine him and shape him through idolatrous images, it's accomplished nothing—less than nothing. Since his image can be seen in his beloved image bearers, image-making is not merely immoral, it's unnecessary. The pure in heart are most apt to see God in their fellow humans, all of which bear his likeness to one degree or another. Granted, it isn't always crystal clear, but the pure hearted are able, not to mention willing, to see past the tarnishing influence of sin in their neighbors to locate and honor what the Latins called the *imago dei*.

Although the image was marred by the fall, it was never erased altogether and is renewed by the Spirit who polishes the stained mirror of the image and gradually restores it to its original brilliance through Jesus. Someone said, "To love one's enemy does not mean to love the mire in which the pearl lies, but to love the pearl that lies in the mire." The purest of hearts see and love that pearl through the mire.

That said, seeing the Lord isn't all goose bumps and giddy feelings. It informs us of his mission and his invitation to join him in it. Moses saw God in the burning bush, David gazed on his "beauty," Isaiah saw him "high and lifted up," and when Paul saw him, like all his pure-hearted predecessors, he signed up for service.

It's not like going to the theater and watching the actors on the screen do all the acting while you gobble your compulsory bucket of buttered popcorn and gulp a large soda. If all God wanted were *fans* instead of *followers* he would've created us as lesser life forms that could only *observe* and not participate. But he's an active God who invites us to work alongside of him.

Jesus saw the Father working and joined him in his work.[4] It takes a pure heart for us to see him at his work and to respond to his invitation to accompany him. Like day laborers in the lumberyard parking lot waiting

---

4. John 5:17, 19.

for an opportunity for an honest day's work, we eager and pure-hearted seers "watch" and wait on the Lord for each day's work assignment.[5]

God hunts for honest hearts to which he can entrust his secrets. He "confides in those who fear him" (Ps 25:14) and "takes the upright into his confidence" (Prov 3:32). He entrusts his secrets and strategies with the pure-hearted so that they may join him in what he is doing in the world.

Pure-Hearted Seers Say What They See

> Therefore, my brothers and sisters, be eager to prophesy. (1 Cor 14:39)

Those with the purest hearts and most socially *upside-down* missions were the prophets of old. From Elijah to Isaiah and Daniel to John the Baptist those fire-bathed, pure-hearted preachers were known as "seers" because they *saw* something and described what they saw. Their descriptions were aimed to bring people into alignment with God's kingdom agenda. They rowed against the current of their day, alerting those sailing merrily by on their way toward disaster downstream.

While it's true that not all kingdom practitioners are *prophets* in the classic sense, those with pure hearts "see" something they can't seem to unsee. They've gazed into God's heart, captured its contents, and can hardly help themselves from sharing it with the outside world. They see God particularly in and among the poor and the marginalized. They recognize him in their struggle to replace the chaos of injustice with the *shalom* of his kingdom and are compelled to speak up.[6]

Seers, then and now, "*speak up* for those who cannot speak for themselves, for the rights of all who are destitute" (Prov 31:8). They don't segregate their moral concerns, but cast down idols *and* call out injustice. Apart from this "prophetic zeal" the church represents something other than our

---

5. Mark 13:37.

6. Speaking of speaking up:
"If anyone sins because they do not *speak up* when they hear a public charge to testify regarding something they have seen or learned about, they will be held responsible." (Lev 5:1)
"Everyone who saw it was saying to one another, 'Such a thing has never been seen or done, not since the day the Israelites came up out of Egypt. Just imagine! We must do something! So *speak up!*'" (Judg 19:30)
"*Speak up* and judge fairly; defend the rights of the poor and needy." (Prov 31:9)

SINGLE-MINDED SEERS

subversive Savior and becomes a "social club without moral or spiritual authority."[7]

Those who *see God* practice both personal purity and social engagement. Splitting the two leads to a warped reading of Scripture and tempts us to domesticate Jesus and his radical kingdom agenda. It's been said that any gospel without feet isn't the gospel at all.

New Testament seers interpret all God-sightings as marching orders. Every glimpse of him in motion becomes their mission. How blessed then are those with an uncluttered heart, who see God at work and are privileged to work alongside him to advance his agenda in the world![8]

---

7. King, "Letter from a Birmingham Jail," para. 33.

8. Andrew Murray was the first person to come to mind regarding purity of heart. Murray, a South African pastor, missionary, and champion of the South African revival in the 1860s, wrote over fifty books. A few that have special meaning to me are *Absolute Surrender*; *Waiting on God*; and *With Christ in the School of Prayer*.

Blessed Are Those Who Make *Shalom*

Blessed are the peacemakers for they will be called the children of God.
—Matt 5:9

If we have no peace, it is because we have forgotten that we belong to each other.
—Mother Teresa

THE BEATITUDES ACT AS a telescope through which we can see and act on what Jesus wants. To the naked eye, kingdom terrain seems unattainably distant. But leaning into the blessed attitudes brings it nearer and, with the help of the Spirit, it becomes more achievable—rather, more *receivable*.

Jesus unfurled the attitudes in an intended sequence wherein one opens the way to the next and so on. Progress in each adjusts the scope for greater clarity of the next. The "poor in spirit" will "mourn" and become "meek" as a result. They will then "hunger and thirst" for transformation, which creates space for increasing "mercy" toward those in need and a sincere ("pure") heart.

We might say that there is scarcely greater evidence of purity than in peacemaking. If people with a pure heart "see" the God of peace it makes perfect sense that they would aspire to become makers of peace.

It's true that our world is a battle zone, but instead of fighting *against* the world, alongside Jesus we fight *for* it. Instead of war, peacemakers wage peace.

The profound polarization in our country (and the world) over race, political party, religion, class, and gender calls for agents of peace, maybe more than ever before. When reporters asked Gandhi what brought about peace between the Indians and the British, he claimed it was the application of the principles of the Sermon on the Mount. May God use his agents of peace today who insist on applying those same principles in America and around the world.

Practitioners of peace are called "children of God" because they remind us of God. He overcomes evil with good, defeats hate by love, and conquers the world by a cross. The Father's family resemblance can be seen through the peacemaking work of sincere, yet still limping lovers of God. By making peace, versus *faking* it, tarnished God-lovers resemble their Father. "If you love peace," says Merton, "then hate injustice, hate tyranny, hate greed–but hate these things in yourself first, not in another."[1]

Follow along as we unpack the privileged purpose of the peacemaker. First, we'll introduce the essence of peacemaking: *shalom*. Next, we'll demonstrate the inseparable connection between peace and justice. Then we'll see that peace is not to be stockpiled but distributed into the world. And lastly, we'll look at the sort of audacity it takes to become a peacemaker.

---

1. Merton, *New Seeds*, 122.

Peace Be with You

While you are proclaiming peace with your lips, be careful to have peace even more fully in your heart.
—Francis of Assisi

I'd kill for a Nobel Peace Prize!
—Steven Wright

Brokering cease-fires and settling disputes is a part, albeit a small part, of the peacemaker's job description.

Paul counseled a couple of women in the Philippian church who were at odds with each other to "iron out their differences and make up" (Phil 4:2, The Message). It's no wonder that he wrote this from eight hundred miles away in the "security" of a Roman prison cell! I've always found the long-distance method to be the safest way, if not the most effective way to mediate disputes between feisty church folk.

As a pastor, whenever I was lured into quarrels between church members and tried to convince them to get along, both warring parties usually ended up redirecting their anger onto me and leaving the church! Not my favorite part of the pastor job.

Mediating disputes and helping people reconcile is a hazardous yet noble task and yet part of the peacemaker's résumé. Fortunately, most of the job is much more life-giving and world-changing than that.

Remember this is not *our* story in which we star, while all the "extras" in the world play off of us. It is the Father's story in which the Spirit directs and Jesus stars. We're his cast, but only in tandem with all our neighbors near and far. We play off of Jesus for his glory and for the good of the rest of the cast. Though we play different parts, recite different lines, are slated for different scenes, none of us are more important than the rest of us to the unfolding story. When the credits roll at the end, all our names will be included in his.

Hence, when a player or groups of players try to hijack the story at the expense of others, instruments of peace step in and say "Not so fast!" They challenge the prima donna's attempt to grab the attention and bring back to the stage those whose roles had been dismissed.

The New Testament Greek term for "peace" (*eirene*) must be folded into the rich Hebrew term used over five hundred times in the Hebrew Bible: *shalom*. You've probably heard it as a greeting; maybe in a song or a sermon, but grasping the thick implications of it dramatically amplifies our understanding of the peacemaker's job description.

Since all of the authors were Jewish (except Luke), virtually all of the references to "peace" in the New Testament harken back to the Hebrew concept of *shalom*. I presume the good doctor had a working knowledge of one of the Hebrew Bible's most significant concepts. In fact, he recorded Mary's prophesy that Jesus would be the one to "guide our feet in the way of shalom."[1]

I admit that I'm obsessed with *shalom*. I like the word, I like how it sounds, and I like what it means. Mostly I love *when it is,* as opposed to when it isn't.

Shalom, like the well-known New Testament Greek term for love—*agape*—can't be contained or explained by a cold and pithy definition. Like agape, we have to *experience shalom* working among people to fully appreciate it. It's not one-dimensional, but has thickness to it. It's as palpable as it is practical.

Shalom is what the kingdom of God looks and sounds and smells like.

As much as I love the word "peace," it's too thin, too tame a term to explain *shalom*. It's like describing the Grand Canyon as "a wide crack in the ground." Though it's true that *shalom* includes what we mean by *peace*, it's just not spacious enough to do it justice. Other good terms like *harmony*, *flourishing*, and *interconnectedness* may drop us off in front of the house of *shalom*, but they still can't quite take us inside to explore its treasures.

If I had to choose one word, one particularly pregnant term, to describe the reality for which God originally fashioned us; that word would

---

1. Luke 1:79, The Tree of Life Version.

be *shalom*. Before the beginning, the Three-in-One enjoyed perfect eternal harmony. At some point (if there is such a thing as a "point" in eternity) they decided to share it with those they created for that very purpose and commissioned them to maintain it. Ever since, *shalom-makers* actively influence the created order toward the vision of the Trinitarian community.

I suspect that if we were to ask God to describe his vision for the world in one word, his answer would be "*Shalom*." *Shalom* is when everything is as it ought to be, a state of full flourishing in every dimension, a comprehensive peace with spiritual, relational, social, political, economic, environmental, and cultural implications. It may be spiritually initiated and psychologically experienced, but essentially *shalom* is earthy, material, and detectible. It's more than euphoric feelings or the interlude between wars. It's the essence of a community at peace with itself.

After he rose from the dead, Jesus said to the disciples, "Peace be with you. As the Father sent me, so I send you." I don't think he meant, *Ya'll feel better now. I'm back!* It was more like, *As you go into the world, be sure to bring shalom with you! Spread it around so everyone can taste and see that it's good!*

Shalom is meant to be both personal, emphasizing our relationships with one another, and structural, improving systems where *shalom* is absent as in greed-driven economic systems. *Shalom-ing* is the work of building interconnectedness around the common good. "Shalom," says Randy Woodley, "is always tested on the margins of society and revealed by how the poor, oppressed, disempowered, and needy are treated."[2]

Racial justice, economic justice, even environmental justice are all included in a *shalom*-filled reality. "Shalom is embedded into the created order and meant to be lived out in the lives of human communities in the broader ecological context."[3] *Shalom* is peace on steroids.

The Creator imagines *shalom* among us and then installs it into our imaginations. Those who wage peace, therefore, work toward a *shalom*-centered society. They experience it and bring it with them wherever they go.

As long as there are constantly hungry people in an otherwise well-fed community there can be no *shalom*. Where there are homeless and jobless people amidst the amply-employed and wealthy, *shalom* isn't. It must be available for everyone in order for anyone to truly enjoy it. It is the biblical

---

2. Woodley, *Shalom and the Community*, 15.
3. Salvatierra, *Faith-Rooted Organizing*, 35.

equivalent of the concept of the "common good." *Shalom* benefits the good of all or it's not *shalom* at all!

Tangle to Tapestry

Think of a *shalom*-filled society as a fabric made of a multitude of interrelated threads, as opposed to a pile of random strands thrown together on the floor. One is a *tapestry* of interconnected people working toward the common good and the other a tangled mess.[4]

Where *shalom* exists, "the threads must be rightly and intimately related to one another in literally a million ways. Each thread must go over, under, around, and through the others at thousands of points."[5] When it doesn't, the fabric tears and its beauty diminishes. When people are elegantly interwoven among one another, you have *shalom*. We call it "community."

Where society is more dis-integrated than integrated, the fabric frays and the weaker members are the first to feel it. *Shalom*-makers insert themselves into the tears in the tapestry and, by the power of the Spirit, reweave the frayed areas. "Reweaving shalom means to sacrificially thread, lace, and press your time, goods, power and resources into the lives and needs of others."[6]

As Martin Luther King said, we all share in the "network of mutuality" and the "garment of destiny." Peacemakers see where the garment is torn, where the network is broken down, and they join with other *shalomers* to repair it to its premeditated beauty.

---

4. I'm indebted to Timothy Keller for this vivid illustration of what *shalom* looks like, how it's compromised, and how it is reclaimed by peacemakers. I encourage the reader to take advantage of his seminal book: *Generous Justice: How God's Grace Makes Us Just*.

5. Keller, Generous Justice, 172.

6. Keller, Generous Justice, 177.

No Justice! No Peace!

I have been gravely disappointed with the [one] who is more devoted to order than to justice; who prefers a negative peace which is the absence of tension to a positive peace which is the presence of justice.

—Martin Luther King Jr.

At some point along the way in most every march or protest I've attended, the chant rises and echoes through the crowd: *No Justice! No Peace! No Justice! No Peace!* Whether or not they realize it, the marchers proclaim a biblical value.

Often mentioned in the same breath by biblical authors, *peace and justice* share a common center and include the other in symbiosis. Where justice is dimmed in a community, *shalom* implodes and vice versa. It makes sense then, that those who "hunger and thirst for justice" make the best peacemakers.

"In the absence of justice," writes Eugene Cho, "we are not truly flourishing; in the absence of justice, shalom is impaired. Shalom goes beyond justice but always includes it. Justice is, you might say, the ground floor of shalom."[1]

For example, when I give talks about human trafficking I often use a metaphor of a sewage-filled river into which coldblooded traffickers shove women and children. For financial gain they throw God's beloveds into a sh**-filled river to suffer and eventually drown. Appalled by such cruelty, mercy-filled people go downstream to pull emotionally comatose casualties out of the river and perform CPR on them.

1. Cho, *Live Justly*, 17.

How do these precious souls find themselves in the sewage to begin with? Who keeps pushing them in and what can we do about it? *Shalom*-makers ask these kinds of questions and then venture *upstream* to address the broken system that allows fiends to ravage the lives of the innocent.

Corazon Aquino is quoted as saying, "While we all hope for peace, it shouldn't be peace at any cost but peace based on principle, on justice." Unity for unity's sake is not necessarily a moral good. Austin Channing Brown once said, "I'm wholly uninterested in a conversation about unity that's not rooted in the unrelenting pursuit of racial justice."

Where injustice remains, unity is just a photo op.

Shalom is tested best on society's margins and is exposed by how the disempowered are treated. When you find an enormous discrepancy between the opportunities for the rich and the poor or for the white and the black or for men and women, *shalom* is AWOL.

The Roman version of peace called the *Pax Romana*, required oppression of the needy by the elite, but God's *shalom* demands justice for the weak and vulnerable.

Systemic injustice is what someone called "violence in slow motion." Jesus' new society challenges the unjust structure, lifts up the oppressed, quells the violence, and restores *shalom*. Peacemakers work for peace by creating the conditions that make anti-peace less likely. Though any *shalom* we achieve here and now is a meager foretaste of *shalom* to come, peacemakers keep their eye on the ultimate prize when someday heaven and earth will once again coalesce.

The *International Justice Mission* says that injustice is "what happens when someone uses their power to take from someone else the good things God intended them to have: their life, their liberty, their dignity, or the fruit of their love or their labor." Where there is obscene inequity and the marginalized are underrepresented, *shalom*-makers disadvantage themselves for the advantage of the disadvantaged.

> If peace means keeping my mouth shut in the midst of injustice and evil, I don't want it. If peace means being complacently adjusted to a deadening status quo, I don't want peace.[2]

Jesus entered into the pain of the disinherited and gave it voice. This is "*Shalom* to Go."

---

2. King, "When Peace Becomes Obnoxious," para. 9. This sermon was delivered on March 18, 1956 at Dexter Avenue Baptist Church.

Shalom to Go

We offer to the world a preview of that future era when Christ rules the new heavens and earth—the era in which all social and cultural realities will be directed toward Christ.

—Bruce Riley Ashford[1]

Shalom is not just for in-house use. Peacemakers take it "to go."

Though there is something to be said for those who *keep the peace*, Jesus' blessing was on peace*makers* not on peace*keepers*. Maintaining the status quo can be done while putting little effort into the advance of the cause of justice. Ours is not a "privatized, minimized, postmortem gospel of how to go to heaven when you die while keeping the world as it has always been."[2] *Peace-practitioners* actively oppose oppression and avidly work for the common good.

Loving peace and making peace aren't the same either. You can love peace and remain content to enjoy it for yourself, while at the same time neglecting the call to advance it in the world.

So, BYOS (Bring Your Own *Shalom*)!

Don't hoard it. Share it. There's plenty of it to go around.

Bringin' It to Babylon!

Circling back to the Hebrew Bible, we find there an avid instigator of *shalom*. In his letter to the exiles in Babylon the prophet Jeremiah

---

1. Ashford, *Every Square Inch*, 20.
2. Zahnd, *Postcards From Babylon*, 77.

recruited other *shalom*-makers and exhorted them to work toward a coherent community in their new temporary home away from home. He urged them as strangers in a strange land to sow *shalom* in Babylonian soil. He exhorted them to lean into God's purpose, which was to make his people better in Babylon and at the same time make Babylon better through his people.

> *"Seek the shalom of the city where I have caused you to be carried away for in the shalom thereof shall ye have shalom.* (Jer 29:7, Orthodox Jewish Bible)

Instead of stockpiling it, instruments of *shalom* bring it with them wherever they go and share it even among their enemies. *Shalom Babylon* and you too will be *shalomed*! We might say today, "Be the *shalom* you want to see."

The opposite is also true: If you hoard *shalom* for yourself instead of sharing it, you're likely to miss it altogether. Sounds quite similar to something Jesus said: "Whoever wants to save their life will lose it, but whoever loses their life for me and for the gospel will save it."[3]

Peter addresses his first epistle to "God's elect, exiles scattered throughout the provinces" and ends it with: "She who is in Babylon, chosen together with you, sends you her greetings."[4] He wants us to connect the dots between the sixth-century BC Jewish exiles in Babylon and ourselves as healing agents in our own foreign culture. We're a hybrid people, citizens of a *shalom*-filled kingdom, and at the same time expatriates dwelling in a foreign land here to weave our king's peace into it.

America (and every other nation for that matter) is a metaphorical extension of Babylon wherein followers of Jesus live as exiles. Babylon AD may or may not be as bad as Babylon BC, but it is our temporary home (away from our eternal home) into which God commissions us to share *shalom*.

While some only concern themselves with *getting themselves the hell out of Babylon*, our mandate is to do our part to *get as much hell out of Babylon* as possible and replace it with the kingdom of heaven. Instead of escaping into spiritual silos, we're to engage with our Babylonian neighbors and nudge them toward the culture of the kingdom. While we refuse to serve Babylon's gods, we do serve the common good of its people.

3. Mark 8:35.
4. 1 Pet 1:1; 5:13.

Part Two | Utterly Upside-Down Attitudes

Jesus doesn't teach us to be *against* the culture, nor to be uncritically *part of* it. Instead, he assigns us to live *in the culture for the sake of the culture*. As ambassadors to Babylon, we're on a *shalom*-making mission.

We take our *shalom* then "to go." We don't leave it locked up in spiritual bomb shelters of our homes or churches because *shalom* doesn't want to stay at home or at church! It breaks out and weaves itself into the tears in the cultural tapestry.

Though perfect *shalom* will only be fully realized at the return of the Prince of *Shalom*, on any given day you can witness peacemakers praying and working for its incremental advance on foreign soil. Their hope is to foment a loving revolution wherein the privileged and powerless flourish together in peace and justice—a preview of the future.

The *Shalom*-Maker's Audacity

Peacemaking doesn't mean passivity. It is the act of interrupting injustice without mirroring injustice, the act of disarming evil without destroying the evil doer, the act of finding a third way that is neither fight nor flight but the careful arduous pursuit of reconciliation and justice.

—Shane Claiborne[1]

What mental picture do you conjure when you hear the word "peacemaker"? A milquetoast with no firm opinions of his own? A mild-mannered mediator who just wants everyone to get along?

Remember, peacemakers aren't all about "keeping the peace." Nor are they necessarily the sort to typically *hold their peace*. Though it may seem counterintuitive, the peacemaker will often be angry enough to do something in love.

Though your Mandelas, Wilberforces, and Martin Luther Kings were peacemaking icons, they often did their best work while under the influence of righteous indignation. Peacemaking and troublemaking are not necessarily antonyms. The late civil rights activist and Congressman John Lewis often spoke about "getting into good trouble." In order to incite *shalom* in the culture, peace practitioners find it necessary to initiate confrontations with the powerful on behalf of the powerless.

Jeremiah called out Israel's poser prophets for their false message: "'Peace, peace' when there is no peace," they preached.[2] Martin Luther King referred to something he called "the devil's peace," which is a counterfeit

---

1. Claiborne, *Common Prayer*, 156.
2. Jer 6:14.

calm that pacifies and lullabies us to doze in deep denial. By way of contrast, King said, "The hope of a secure and livable world lies with disciplined nonconformists who are dedicated to justice, peace, and brotherhood."[3]

Sometimes peacemakers have to become sufficiently exasperated at injustice in order to rankle other people enough to acknowledge their complicity in it. I'm not suggesting that it's our task to infect the atmosphere with contempt. The best *shalom*-makers, though audacious, are nothing if not humble as well as civil. They are anything but passive, yet nothing if combative. "Wise as serpents and harmless as doves."[4]

Never in my lifetime has our country been so polarized as it is today. Certain preachers, pundits, and politicians armed with especially vitriolic rhetoric appeal to, if not incite, the basest of human emotions in some of our more naïve church members and citizens. Such leaders contribute to a culture void of *shalom*.

Shalom cannot be dictated or imposed. "My kingdom is not of this world," says Jesus. "If it were, my servants would fight."[5] He tasks us to fight *for peace*, not to pick fights with those who try to prevent it. Remember it's the *meek* that inherit the earth.

That said, making peace is not about pretending everything is oakie dokie or convincing everyone to overlook injustice in the world. "So often the contemporary Church is a weak, ineffectual voice with an uncertain sound," wrote Martin Luther King. "So often it is an arch defender of the status quo. Far from being disturbed by the presence of the Church, the power structure of the average community is consoled by the church's silent—and often even vocal—sanction of things as they are."[6]

In order for *shalom* to flourish, we have to do the hard work of breaking up the fallow ground and pulling the weeds in the cultural soil.[7] Making peace may require making some enemies. When it does, all is not lost, unless we fail to love our enemies as Jesus taught us to.[8]

---

3. King, *Strength to Love*, 48.
4. Matt 10:16.
5. John 18:36.
6. From King, "Letter from a Birmingham Jail," 32..
7. Jer 4:3.
8. To my mind, a great *shalom*-maker in his time was William Wilberforce, the British member of parliament and leader in the movement to abolish the slave trade in the United Kingdom. For an accurate yet entertaining depiction of his life, I recommend the movie, *Amazing Grace*.

The Shalom-Maker's Audacity

Peacemakers are bold prophetic troublemakers yet civil of tongue, a plucky but loving sort. They're audacious yet humble servants of God and people, who make "good trouble" in order to inspire the culture to change course and make adjustments in unjust systems. Some will do just that, while others will object and push back—some with words, others with fists, which brings us to our final Beatitude.

The Empire Strikes Back

Blessed are those who are persecuted because of righteousness, for theirs is the Kingdom of heaven. Blessed are you when people insult you, persecute you and falsely say all kinds of evil against you because of me. Rejoice and be glad, because great is your reward in heaven, for in the same way they persecuted the prophets who were before you.

—MATT 5:10-12

Jesus promised his disciples three things–that they would be completely fearless, absurdly happy, and in constant trouble.

—G. K. CHESTERTON

The Last Beatitude

AS YOU KNOW BY now, we've been inching our way through what I believe is a sequence of Beatitudes. We've finally arrived at what might be the most bewildering one of the eight.[1] This is where Jesus disabuses us of the notion that following him is the best way to be safe from all harm and makes us everyone's BFF.

Persecution is the price we pay for living the way Jesus lays out in his Address and part of what Dietrich Bonheoffer called, "the cost of discipleship." Martin Luther King Jr. wrote, "Cowardice asks the question, 'Is it safe?'

---

1. Some interpreters break this Beatitude into two, one to the crowd ("Blessed are *they who* . . . ") and the other to his disciples ("Bless are *you when* . . . "). The one has to do with physical persecution and the other about slander. I see them more as two parts of the same thing, and rather than nine, my take is that he gave eight beatitudes, this being the last.

Expediency asks the question, 'Is it politic?' Vanity asks the question, 'Is it popular?' But conscience asks the question, 'Is it right?' And there're times when you must take a stand that is neither safe nor politic nor popular, but you must do it because it is right."[2]

This last Beatitude is different from the others in that it issues a warning about the repercussions of choosing to embody the other seven. It's what happens when we acknowledge our spiritual poverty, grieve it, are meek about it, and so on.[3] You know the drill by now.

Yet, in contrast to the others, Jesus prescribes a certain attitude to persecuted kingdom-ites: *joy and gladness,* in spite of—if not because of—the opposition we face.

It's not as though we seek ill treatment for our faith, yet such treatment is part of the requisite for entering the race. We're not masochists who, in order to vaunt our spirituality, revel in rejection and repulse others on purpose in order to garner as much of their disapproval as possible. The gospel carries with it its own offense and doesn't need us to contribute to it by being foolish. Some Christians earn others' contempt by ridiculous messaging and hypocritical lifestyles. In such cases, since it can't really be called *persecution*, there aren't any *blessings* attached to it.

Notice that the consequence of this last Beatitude is the same as the first: "theirs is the Kingdom of heaven." What he had in mind was more of a cycle than a one-off set of eight steps one takes. In this life we never achieve perfect humility, meekness, purity, or the ability to make peace. But as we lean into each attitude, we find ourselves more deeply ensconced in the next one and so on. And then we engage in repeated immersions in poverty of spirit, only to mourn it in order to increase our meek spirit and to hunger for more surpassing righteousness. It's not linear, but cyclical until we someday finish our race and cast our crowns at his feet.

A Punch in the Nose

Though I have been threatened on account of my faith a few times, the only incident in which I was actually physically assaulted for it was back when I

---

2. Washington, *Testament of Hope,* 268.

3. As I said, the first seven attitudes cause the attitude-holders to be persecuted. But it's equally true that the seven are the qualities we need in order to face our persecutions with grace. Humility, lament, meekness, mercy, purity are the means by which endure the treatment we receive from our detractors.

was in college in Southern California. One late night after our shift at UPS a friend and I stood next to our cars talking when three menacing drunk guys dressed in gang attire approached us with a request, actually more of a demand, for a ride to the liquor store. All that my imagination could conjure was being clubbed over the head from the back seat and losing my car. So, I decided the best course was to strike up a conversation with them in hopes that they'd forget their plan and go on their inebriated merry way.

It didn't work as well as I had envisioned. They weren't going anywhere anytime soon, so, I figured if we couldn't wear them down with chitchat, I'd take advantage of the opportunity to share Christ with them.

As I began, the one I was talking with told me that he didn't need to hear it since he was already a Christian. I insinuated that in light of his apparent lifestyle I seriously doubted the genuineness of his confession. (Please cut me a little slack, as I was a stupid nineteen-year-old new believer.) Well, he didn't take my valuation of his faith in stride and hauled off and belted me in the face!

One of the other two took umbrage at his partner's misdeed, and handed me his bandana to soak up the blood pouring out of my nose.

I took up a conversation with Drunk Guy #2 and, wouldn't you know, the theme mirrored the first one. I told him he needed Christ. He claimed to have as much religion as he needed. (Remember what I said above about being a stupid kid and new at this.) When I challenged him, just like the first guy, he punched me! (Since both punches landed pretty straight up on my nose, I don't know if any of it qualified as a bona fide cheek-turning opportunity.)

My friend, by the way, was unmolested throughout the entire ordeal. I think he was smart enough to tone down his testifying and go with a kinder, gentler approach. But I was getting tired of getting slugged, so I told them to climb in and dropped them off at the nearest liquor store.

Of course, I bragged to everyone at my college dorm about what a martyr for Christ I was! In hindsight, it was more like *ignorant for Christ*, but it was a long time ago, so maybe my recollection of it isn't entirely accurate.

What I do know is that I might have avoided a sore nose and a bloody shirt had I remembered what Jesus said about the folly of trying to get certain people to accept our "pearls" of wisdom before they're ready.[4] He warned us that failure to adhere to his counsel on such matters would result

---

4. Matt 5:7.

in being "trampled" and "torn to pieces." I get it now, though! Always a day late and a dollar short.

So, Christianity is not a pain reliever and though the shield of faith quenches Satan's flaming darts, it doesn't necessarily keep us from getting punched in the nose!

Our Persecuted Prototype

> A servant is not greater than his master. If they persecuted me, they will persecute you also. (John 15:20)

If they persecuted our Leader, how could we, who aspire to live in lock step with him, expect anything other for ourselves?

Have you seen those small boxes containing cards with Bible promises for each day of the year? I'd venture to guess that not many promises of persecution are included in them.

God doesn't promise perpetual safety and comfort. In fact, it's often quite the opposite.[5] From Jesus' narrow escape during the "Massacre of the Innocents" in Bethlehem when he was two years old, to his brutal execution in Jerusalem thirty-plus years later, the power brokers of the empire and their collaborators relentlessly struck back on him. If they persecuted the Master, how can his servants escape?

"American Christians need to stop feeling at home," Stanley Hauerwas is reported to have said. "We thought that we had created a culture in which people were at last safe to be Christians. That was a mistake. . . . By being adopted to be part of a journey called discipleship, Christians are permanently ill at ease in the world." True followers of the Christ of the Mount must get used to the sight of their own blood.

So, it's no shock when the empire strikes back! When they reject us, insult us, punch us in the nose, or worse, they're simply reminding us that we don't technically belong here. This place is not our permanent home. We

---

5. "In this world you will have trouble . . . " (John 16:33).

"You will be handed over to be persecuted and put to death, and you will be hated by all nations because of me" (Matt 24:9).

"Truly I tell you, no one who has left home or brothers or sisters or mother or father or children or fields for me and the gospel will fail to receive a hundred times as much in this present age: homes, brothers, sisters, mothers, children and fields—along with persecutions—and in the age to come eternal life." (Mark 10:29–30)

PART TWO | UTTERLY UPSIDE-DOWN ATTITUDES

are citizens of a kingdom that is so unlike this one that if they don't *join us* they're as likely as not to *jeer us* instead.

The idea that the world exists to serve us is a narcissistic myth. We're not here just to enjoy Babylon's benefits. Rather, as marginalized exiles in a foreign land, we're here to reach Babylonians and to work toward a shift in their culture.

In the following chapters we'll distinguish *true* persecution from false, speak to why they object to Christianity to begin with, and identify what Jesus prescribes by way of response.

Persecution: When It Is and When It Isn't

When martyrdom is no longer considered a possibility, we turn Christianity into a safe and anodyne civil religion in service of the empire.

—Brian Zahnd[1]

In 2001 I taught for a short time in a small Bible College in Tel Aviv. Most of the students were Nigerian pastors, who were in Israel to escape persecution and to make some money to send home to their families. I used the 2 Corinthians Epistle as a backdrop to teach about spiritual leadership in the face of opposition. About halfway through the first day it became obvious that they knew lightyears more about persecution up close and personal than I ever had and probably ever will.

Those saintly men had seen family and friends beaten, jailed, and some put to death for their faith. They had personally been threatened and assaulted for their role as pastors, and here I was teaching *them* about persecution! Once I finally paused long enough to hear their stories, we proceeded to use most of the rest of the time praying for them, their families, and their congregations back home.

Most of us Western Christians have little to no personal experience with actual persecution. Without realizing our own privileged position in our culture, what we call "persecution" is often no more than a slap on the wrist—as opposed to a slug in the face.

As multitudes of our brothers and sisters in other countries are thrown in prison or killed by their own family members for their faith in Christ,

---

1. Zahnd, *Postcards From Babylon*, 74.

millions of Americans cry "Persecution!" over things like temporary partial shutdowns of in-person church services during the pandemic. We can't even seem to bear harsh tweets from people who are at odds with us about politics, let alone bear the ire of the empire.

When the boss prohibits a "Merry Christmas" greeting at the office water cooler, it's not persecution. Persecution would be getting thrown in jail for it. Removing prayer from public schools or taking down the Ten Commandments from courthouse walls is mild by comparison with the real thing. Outlawing prayer in our homes or banning sermons on the Ten Commandments in our churches would be another story.

"Evangelicalism," says Carlos A. Rodríguez, "has abandoned self-sacrifice and replaced it with a persecution complex that expects others to sacrifice themselves for the sake of Evangelicalism." A lot of Christians are like the guy who said, "The only reason I'm paranoid is because everyone's against me!"

Appealing to their Christian base, some politicians run campaigns on the loss of "religious liberty" as though *our* faith is the only one worth protecting, and that if we don't protect it, Christianity will be wiped off the face of the earth in one generation. When I think of all the people who have lost their lives for the gospel over the last twenty centuries it seems disrespectful to compare their suffering with our petty beefs with those who don't like us much.

What many of us call *persecution* is but a tame facsimile of the real thing. As we retreat into our spiritual safe houses, incessantly groan about our godless culture, and insist on our privileges, we signal where our treasure actually lies.

Americans are so used to our nation as *pro-Christian* that we've come to expect special treatment. And if we don't receive it, we interpret every minor loss of privilege as persecution. While we thought we possessed "home team advantage," with our fans out-cheering those on the other side, it turns out that we're actually, and always have been, the "away team"— *strangers and foreigners*—in this world.

The "Un-Persecutable"

Some Christians suffer because they are insufferable. Jesus pronounced blessing upon those who are persecuted for their righteousness, not for their *foolishness*. Persecution is only "blessed" if its cause is legitimate and the persecuted are virtuous. "Sometimes the world rejects Christians because it rejects Christ," says David French. "Sometimes, however, the world rejects Christians because Christians are cruel. In that case, alienation isn't persecution. It represents righteous judgment for our own political sin."[2]

The anti-kingdom demands conformity. Anything less and it will penalize us. The only way to avoid it is to be its echo.

"Woe to you," says Jesus, "when everyone speaks well of you."[3] "Woe" is in effect the counter to "blessed." *Blessed* are you if you're persecuted and *woe* to you if you're not. Talk about an upside-down kingdom!

By persecuting us they're just telling us that we don't belong. At least they get that right. Jesus told his half-brothers that there was no threat of them being persecuted, as they were too much like everyone else.[4]

It's the unsalty salt that gets "trampled" like road dust, dismissed as a non-entity. Worse than being persecuted is to be ignored altogether. Wouldn't you say that it's a whole lot better to have them mad at us than bored with us?

"One wonders why Christians today get off so easily," writes Clarence Jordan.[5] "Is it because unchristian Americans are that much better than unchristian Romans, or is our light so dim that the tormentor cannot see it? What are the things we do that are worth persecuting?"

Following Jesus isn't necessarily *safe,* nor does it mean we won't even be killed for his sake. But it does mean he'll be with us in our suffering and reward us in this life and certainly in the next.

---

2. French, "Why Do They Hate Us?," para. 29.

3. Luke 6:26.

4. John 7:7.

5. Jordan, who helped found Habitat for Humanity and also founded Koinonia, a collective farm in Georgia that employed and served poor African Americans in the 1940s, was sorely persecuted for his kingdom faith. The KKK burned crosses on his property, bombed his farm a number of times, shot at him and his children with machine guns, and threatened anyone who supported his work. An arsonist threw a pillow soaked in gasoline into the home of one of the farm's black employees and burnt down the house. When Jordan died in 1969 the white coroner refused to come to the farm, so a friend had to transport his body into town in his station wagon.

When asked about everything the community did to scare him out of their town, he said, "Shall we go off and leave them without hope? If it costs us our lives, if we must be hung on a cross to redeem our brothers and sisters in the flesh, so be it. It will be well worth it."

PART TWO | UTTERLY UPSIDE-DOWN ATTITUDES

Christians who pose no threat to the status quo, whose lives and message bear no resemblance to the culture of kingdom are seldom candidates for actual persecution.

> A church that doesn't provoke any crises, a gospel that doesn't unsettle, a word of God that doesn't get under anyone's skin or touch the real sin of the society in which it is being proclaimed—what gospel is that?[6]

---

6. El Salvadoran martyr, Father Oscar Romero.

Why Are They So Mad At Us?

That's how they persecuted the prophets who were before you.
—MATTHEW 5:12

Persecuted Prophets

NO DOUBT YOU'VE NOTICED from your reading in the Old Testament that prophets are seldom voted Homecoming Kings or Queens. They lived an upside-down lifestyle, preached an unpopular message, and were penalized for it.

As I said before, it seems that Jesus insinuated an intended correspondence between those firebrand spokesmen of old and us who hear, speak, and do the works of God today.[1] If we were to act in our day as subversively as they did in theirs, we would be well advised to expect some serious blow back. If, like them, we speak truth to (and about) power it's a lock to at least get us on somebody's "Don't Invite to Parties" list.

Jeremiah was marginalized, beaten, tossed in a cistern, and jailed. They pitched Daniel into a den of hungry lions and his three friends into a blazing incinerator. John the Baptizer had his head severed from his body. Others were "stoned, sawed in two, or slain by sword. They wandered in deserts, lived in caves and holes in the ground."[2] How is it that we, who follow in their footsteps expect VIP treatment from our post-Christian culture?

---

1. This is not to be confused with the "office" of prophet (Eph 4:11–12) or even the gift of prophecy mentioned in 1 Cor 12:9 and Rom 12:6. While we're not all prophets in the technical sense, on some level God wants us all to live and serve the world prophetically (1 Cor 14:5, Num 11:29).

2. Heb 11:37.

Of course, people object to our preaching to them about a God they can't see or touch. They feel threatened that we don't get plastered with them on the weekends, refuse to chuckle at their racist jokes, and take our leave before the stripper arrives at the bachelor party. But it's more than our commitment to *personal purity* that irks those who reject our gospel. It's our norm-shattering truth-telling that gets us into holy trouble.

They persecute prophets. If they're mad at us, it could very well be because we follow in the steps of those agitators of old. If they're not mad, it might be that we've lost sight of the footprints that the prophets intentionally left for us to walk in.

Jesus dubs us "the light of the world." You'd think the world would appreciate a little illumination to prevent having to stumble around in the dark. However, people prefer the cover of darkness in order to get away with their bad behaviors.[3] One reason people object to our gospel is that it opens the blinds, lets in the sun's rays, and exposes their sin.[4]

Before I came to Jesus, my girlfriend brought me to a Christian concert. I was fine until the lights came on at intermission, and with my cover blown it felt like all five hundred people in attendance gazed directly into my soul. The only way to get it to stop was to get up, walk out, and hitch a ride home!

Preserving Privilege

Jesus and his merry band of followers were always irritating Jewish and Roman powerbrokers. Eventually, they executed Jesus, Peter, and Paul, "not for their religious beliefs about an afterlife, but because the kingdom of heaven that they announced and enacted posed a challenge to the dominant myth that Rome had a manifest destiny to rule the nations and a divine right to shape history."[5] Sound familiar?

What about the Jewish leaders? What threat did Jesus pose to them? His claim to be God wasn't exactly the most effective campaign strategy ever devised. He drew larger crowds than the religious experts. His theology was much less predictable than theirs and he spurned many of their tidy traditions. But the leaders had another even more potent motive for marginalizing and eventually lynching him.

3. John 3:19.
4. Eph 5:13.
5. Zahnd, *Postcards From Babylon*, 11.

Why Are They So Mad At Us?

Those supposed spiritual leaders were in cahoots with Rome and quite enjoyed the perks and privileges afforded them. They wrangled their countrymen to stay in line with their occupiers, forcing them to pay exorbitant taxes to support their opulent lifestyle. Though they despised the brutal Roman regime, they looked the other way when it benefitted them, and would do whatever it took to quell even a hint of altering the system that served them so well.

As Jesus' popularity grew, they said, "If we let him go on, pretty soon everyone will be believing in him and the Romans will come and remove what little power and privilege we still have."[6] The high priest, in order to retain his power, thought it "expedient"[7] to assassinate the iconoclastic Troublemaker. With their income, influence, and privilege at stake, from that day forward the religious elite plotted his murder.

They objected to him as he refused to keep some of their traditions and preach their religion. More than that, his presence was a threat to the privileged status quo they had come to enjoy.

Persecuted Peacemakers

How is it that *peacemakers* (the Beatitude just prior to this one) are possibly the most apt to be *persecuted*?

Custodians of the status quo are less than fond of those who contend for *shalom*, as they stand to lose the most if *shalom* is actuated. Those who labor to even out the playing field will never achieve favorite-friend status with those whose lifestyles are tied to the field remaining uneven.

Those who engage in bringing peaceful interconnectedness into a social order that thrives on disconnection are the most likely targets of harassment. *Shalom wreckers* hold on to their privilege with a grip that would embarrass a pit bull.

Social symbiosis is not the friend of the ruling class. There couldn't be any two things less compatible than their exploitive way of conducting business and the new society that Jesus proposed. His kingdom drives a peace treaty through the heart of their war.

Want to irk those who think of themselves as *in charge?* Suggest that there is someone quite a bit higher up the organizational chart than them. Want to stir the ire of the powerful? Preach a gospel that diffuses power

6. John 11:48, The Message.
7. John 11:50.

among the powerless. Those with power to spare tend not to be enthusiastic about sharing it. They object to others being made "equal" to them "who have borne the burden of the work and the heat of the day."[8]

Empires run on status, while Jesus chooses poor fishermen, prostitutes, and failed revolutionaries. Those who claim special status for themselves and their tribe resent the notion of social equity. Therefore, they reject the message and persecute the messengers.

Why are they so mad at us? Because Jesus' Kingship disrupts the norms to which they're so accustomed, and when it does, people (and demons) get upset. They lash out, sometimes in insults and accusations. And in more severe cases, with threats, injustice, a punch in the nose, or much worse.

If they actually are mad at us, it's because we propose that Someone else is in charge and his kingdom trumps all the other kingdoms of this world.

---

8. Matthew 20:12

So, What Do We Do About It?

You're blessed when your commitment to God provokes persecution. The persecution drives you even deeper into God's kingdom. Not only that—count yourselves blessed every time people put you down or throw you out or speak lies about you to discredit me. What it means is that the truth is too close for comfort and they are uncomfortable. You can be glad when that happens—give a cheer, even!—for though they don't like it, I do! And all heaven applauds. And know that you are in good company. My prophets and witnesses have always gotten into this kind of trouble.

—Matt 5:10–12, The Message

How do we arrive at blessedness when being persecuted?

Lean Further into the Upside-Down Lifestyle

Persecution drives you even deeper into God's Kingdom.

Not to belittle the severe suffering that millions of godly people have endured for Christ, but the pain of persecution can be considered an ally when it helps us recognize and resist our true enemies: sin, Satan, and the system of the world. And it may even prompt us to live more deeply in the way of Jesus. Suffering of all sorts, including persecution can, with the Spirit's help, bring out the best in us.

The martyrs of old weren't killed for killing others but were killed for loving them. Are we secure enough in who we are in Jesus to turn the other cheek? If we are, we'll pass the persecution tests with grace and forgiveness.

We'll be able to resist "resisting the evil person" and love our enemies that seek to shame us, if not harm us.

Wouldn't our detractors just love it if we gave up our pursuit of what's right? Yet far from reneging on our allegiance to live as citizens of his subversive kingdom, we can actually be "glad" about the pressure they put on us. In truth, our persecutors' unintended consequence crowds us to Christ! And instead of *caving in,* we may just find ourselves *digging in* to meekness, a craving for justice, mercy, purity, and peacemaking. Instead of becoming *bitter* at our detractors we may actually become *better* disciples.

As soon as we stop expecting our culture to roll out the red carpet for us and throw us a welcome party, we may actually come to embrace our identity as "aliens and strangers" here. In the same way that the sixth-century exiles steeled themselves in order to bring *shalom* to their new digs in Babylon,[1] we may press into the *beatitudinal* lifestyle as *salt and light* among our contemporary Babylonians.

Love and Pray for Your Persecutors

> Love your enemies and pray for those who persecute you. (Matt 5:44)

Instead of demonizing our persecutors (like they do us), Jesus teaches us to love and to bless them. He modeled this spirit at his execution: "Father forgive them!"

> To retaliate with hate and bitterness would do nothing but intensify the hate in the world. Along the way of life, someone must have sense enough and morality enough to cut off the chain of hate. This can be done only by projecting the ethics of love to the center of our lives.[2]

Jesus pointed out the madness of putting a "lamp under a bowl," which, in addition to extinguishing the light, could do something worse if the bowl is flammable! Yet some, whose faith is all about their own safety, insist on hunkering down in sheltered Christian bunkers within cozy proximity to their circle of Christian friends and family to wait it out until Jesus

---

1. Jer 25:7.

2. Martin Luther King in a 1957 article for the *Christian Century* called "Nonviolence and Racial Justice" (para. 14).

parts the clouds. Those who love their enemies have a higher priority than their own *comfort and survival*.

Though our Babylon can be a precarious place for us whose citizenship is elsewhere, we resist the temptation to construct a cultural wall and hide behind it. We won't live in fear, for our mission is to love and influence Babylonians toward our kng and his kingdom. Playing perpetual defense or concocting an impenetrable Christian subculture to safeguard ourselves from contamination and persecution is not an option for us.

It's hard to pray for people and hate them at the same time. When we pray for those who hate us (and our gospel) we tap into a love that comes from outside us and gradually works its way inside.

So, if we choose to follow the way of Jesus as prescribed in the Sermon we may well wind up on a cross, like him. "But fortunately, crucifixions have a way of being followed by resurrections."[3]

Look Forward and Dance

> Rejoice and be glad, because great is your reward in heaven. (Matt 5:12)

That which awaits us in the best of all places puts our present persecution in perspective and renders it bearable. Two months before he was assassinated, Martin Luther King encouraged his brethren by preaching, "We must accept finite disappointment, but never lose infinite hope!"

Jesus was no politician, sequestering himself safe and secure in a boardroom far from the battlefield while sending young soldiers to their death. He "endured the cross for the joy that was set before him"[4] and his associates followed suit and rejoiced in the privilege of joining him in the "fellowship of his sufferings." Knowing there is a reward to come, they "delighted in weaknesses, in insults, in hardships, in persecutions, in difficulties."[5]

As someone said, "Faith is hearing the music and hope is dancing to it."

3. Jordan, *Sermon on the Mount*, 89.
4. Heb 12:2.
5. 2 Cor 12:10.

So, when you're insulted or even hated for your faith you might not feel like dancing a jig (or any other kind of dance for that matter). But hopefully, just knowing that persecution is more the *norm* for the Christian, and that the persecuted are "blessed," will help you respond to it in the right spirit.

And if you never experience persecution of any kind, I hope that you'll measure the depth of your faith in Christ and ask him to take you deeper.

Now that we've journeyed through some of the social implications of Jesus' great Message, round the corner with me to the final lap of our study, where he calls us to take action. Here in his concluding remarks, he invites us to incorporate his wise yet radical ideas into our daily lives.

Part Three

WHAT ON EARTH?

Don't look for shortcuts to God. The market is flooded with surefire, easygoing formulas for a successful life that can be practiced in your spare time. Don't fall for that stuff, even though crowds of people do. The way to life—to God!—is vigorous and requires total attention.

—MATT 7:13–14, THE MESSAGE

THE BEST SERMONS HAVE good conclusions that provoke us to take action. Loath to give the impression that he taught merely to *inform*, Jesus invested a large portion of his Sermon to his concluding remarks. As all good preachers, he preached for change, to *transform* the hearts and therefore the lifestyles of his hearers.

The thing that often haunted me after preaching was the fear that my audience would not *act* on what I had done my best to preach. Would they *internalize* it or merely be content to analyze its contents? Would they invite God's words like seeds into their hearts or let them remain on the surface, fair game for the evil one to come and snatch away?[1]

Some call it an "invitation," a "come-to-Jesus moment," or an "altar call." Call it whatever you like, but Jesus compels us to apply what he taught, to reorder our lives appropriate to his kingdom from heaven.

---

1. Matt 13:19.

His Sermon and this book and have something in common. They both ask the central question: *What on earth?* What are we doing on earth if not to inject it with a healthy dose of kingdom? Otherwise, as soon as we say yes to him he would snatch us out of this world and take us to the better one.

Jesus' Greatest Hits aren't so much about the *next world.* Instead, he challenges us to confront the inherently diseased status quo of the world we currently inhabit. Has he not commissioned us to partner with him in his project of moving the cultural needle in the direction of his better-world paradigm? If so, it will actually require *doing* what he says.

His Manifesto shows us how to steward our lives in such a way that his heaven-saturated kingdom will seep into earth's cracks. The Beatitudes that frame his message are *attitudes* that must lead to *actions.*

Kingdom life is accessed through a "narrow gate" that leads to a "narrow path." While there's no entrance fee per se, in order to walk this narrow path, our egotism, affluenza, and our merciless independence must be sacrificed.

Not everyone is willing to divest themselves of their oversized baggage to travel this narrow way. Yet we cannot hold on to *our way* and walk in *his way* at the same time. Calling him "Lord" is no magical *open sesame* for immediate access to his abundance.[2] Nor does doubling it to, "Lord, Lord!" make it any more effective unless we actually submit to his lordship.[3]

We can and must pray for his kingdom to come and his will to be done on earth as it is in heaven. But never forget that in order for *his kingdom to come, our kingdom must go.* Until we surrender our will to his, we can't rightly claim his friendship, let alone his Lordship. It's a *narrow* path.

His invitation is heavy with metaphors—*gates, fruit trees, and building contractors.* It's like squeezing through a narrow aperture, like a tree bearing nourishing fruit, and like a house atop solid rock.

---

2. Evidently, confessing "Jesus is Lord" in order to be saved (Rom 10:9) means something much more than saying the words.

3. Matt 7:21–22.

Walk the Narrow Road

Enter through the narrow gate. For wide is the gate and broad is the road that leads to destruction, and many enter through it. But small is the gate and narrow the road that leads to life, and only a few find it.

—Matt 7:13–14

What is it that makes the kingdom road so narrow?

Though healthy doctrine is crucial, it's not theological purity at issue here. This isn't about how many Bible verses we can recite or what we believe about the Trinity or the Second Coming. What determines outcomes is, in addition to what we believe about his teaching, whether or not we choose to act on what he taught. What makes it so *narrow* is the challenge of following him in the path of obedience.

Love and bless the most nightmarish people in your life, demolish the idol called "Mammon" in your heart, jump for joy when your goodness makes people hate you, and treat others the way you want to be treated. *That's a narrow road!* It's trying to squeeze through the gate with all our excess baggage in tow that makes the way seem so impenetrably narrow. No wonder so "few find it."

Let's be clear. Jesus is not talking about how to get to heaven. He doesn't say anything about heaven here. Instead, he says this road leads "to life." As we walk further down the narrow path, it gradually opens up to the vast expanse of what life was meant to be, both here and eventually in the hereafter.

In another place he said: "It is easier for a camel to go through the eye of a needle than for someone who is rich to enter the Kingdom of God."[1] Though I claim no extensive knowledge on desert-dwelling dromedaries, I do know that they don't fit nicely through needles' eyes. They're simply too big to be shoved through small openings, especially with that big bump on their backs!

The thing that makes Jesus' hyperbole that much more "hyperboleous" is the fact that these mammals can survive long periods of time in arid environments without food or drink because they save up surplus resources in their humps. They're already too big for narrow openings, but consider that awkward bump on their backs, not to mention those born with two protuberances, and the metaphor just gets silly. It takes no graduate degree in zoology to reason that the bigger the hump the more difficult it would be to squeeze through a needle's eye! If he'd been preaching at another time in another part of the world, Jesus might've said, "It's easier to push an elephant through a garden hose."

Living *beatitudinally* reduces our massive egos so we can fit through the tight gate and travel the narrow road. The road is just the right width to accommodate those who mourn their spiritual poverty, the meek who thirst for justice, the merciful and pure-hearted peacemakers.

It's not the "hearers" but the "doers of the word"[2] that bring the king's justice to earth. There isn't room enough for both *your way* and *his way* on the narrow way. Some things just have to be left behind.

The Broad Way

Richard Rohr says, "The broad way is conventional wisdom . . . collective sleepwalking . . . the predictable paths of religious, economic and political cultures."[3] The broad way is small on sacrifice and big on self-rule. You can make up your religion as you go and live your own preferences if you want. But that way ultimately, if not immediately, reduces the possibility for you to experience God's way. Many travel that road, and few walk the other. It's your choice to make.

I had a fifth-grade teacher named Mrs. Hedgland. One day as we were doing long division or fractions or some such thing, I raised my hand and

---

1. Matt 19:24.
2. Jas 1:22.
3. Rohr, *Jesus' Plan*, 132.

suggested an easier way to go about it, at which she was clearly irked. (This was neither the first nor the last time I got under her flabby skin.) She shot back, "Barney Wiget, are you always looking for the easy way?"

Perplexed, I paused and said, "Well . . . yeah." I couldn't imagine the point in doing something the *hard way* when there's an easier one available. Especially with recess just around the corner, I was looking for something to move this thing along a little quicker. The easier the better has always been my mantra!

Broad Road Religion is the easy way. You don't have to give up anything or change any behaviors. Say a sinner's prayer, and you're good to go. You can be anything, do anything, express yourself in any way you decide, and God will be happy just to have your company! In this case, the *easy way* is definitely not *the better way*.

The broad way is a self-centered, self-aggrandizing way. Though many people choose it because they assume it benefits *them*, they stand little chance of improving themselves or the world, and often don't even care to try. (Their light is dim and their salt unsalty.) If you go that way, you'll likely have lots of company, as it is roomy enough for "many" to travel, along with whatever excess baggage you want to bring along for the trip.

The broad way isn't the kingdom way and won't lead you where your heart of hearts wants to be. Its selective sanctification neither pleases God nor fills your soul. Only narrow-way travellers obtain *shalom* and distribute it.

Unfortunately, there is never a shortage of *broad-way preachers* who are quite happy to show you the broad way and take you along for the ride.

Stay Clear of Broad-Way Preachers

Watch out for false prophets. They come to you in sheep's clothing, but inwardly they are ferocious wolves.

—Matt 7:15

Sometimes the Bible in the hand of one man is worse than a whisky bottle in the hand of [another].

(Harper Lee, *To Kill a Mockingbird*)

Preachers of the broad way deny that the kingdom path is narrow and, like carnival barkers, they attract the unwary toward the road that leads to destruction. For their own popularity and prosperity these wolves reduce Jesus' instructions down to suggestions. They convince their disciples that the way is not so narrow and can be entered and enjoyed without having to leave anything behind.

Many broad-way preachers simply bid us to hide out in our comfy Christian culture till God whisks us away to a far, far better place with no concern for making this world a better place. Some err either by exclusively handing out tickets to heaven while evading the social consequences of the kingdom or they preach a "social gospel" that has no redemptive power to transform hearts.

Others actually advocate taking over the world by any means necessary, including, in some cases, by violent overthrow, thus rebutting Jesus' first-tier command to love, bless, and pray for our enemies. Each of these is at cross-purposes with the inverted kingdom Jesus both preached on the mount and modeled in the valley.

Stay Clear of Broad-Way Preachers

Their seductive version of Christianity might gather a crowd and make its preachers a bunch of ready cash, but it's anything but "beatitudinal." "Outwardly they look like sheep, but inwardly they are only thinking about eating sheep!"[1]

These false preachers, pundits, and politicians come in all shapes, sizes, and spiritual grifts. Some are hyper-religious, some are barely religious, and others are irreligious altogether. What they have in common is that they all call people to a kingdom that bears no resemblance to the one from heaven. Their message does more to add to their fame and fortune than it does to cultivate personal and social transformation. Their mantra is, *Follow me as I follow me.*

Through the good prophet Jeremiah, God warned of such preachers who "do not benefit these people in the least," who "run with their own message," and "prophesy the delusions of their own minds" (Jer 23:21, 25, 32).

"Did we not prophesy in your name," they will say to the Lord, "and in your name drive out demons and in your name perform many miracles?" (Matt 7:22). They engage in a form of *identity theft,* as they misuse Jesus' name to captivate their audiences. They might call him "Lord," preach stirring sermons, and even do miracles, none of which legitimizes them or their ministries.

Sadly, many churchgoers whose naiveté is well-documented and whose discern-o-meters are broken or buried under years of listening to broad-way sermons, travel that road with impunity. They gravitate toward whatever scratches their itch for an easier kingdom path.[2] In their preoccupation with the spectacular they lose sight of emulating the character of Christ and ignore his kingdom way to redeem their hearts and renovate the world.

Some may be orthodox in their theology and lead impressive organizations yet do everything but follow Jesus. They don't mourn their poverty of spirit. They aren't meek. They don't hunger for justice, show mercy, have pure hearts, or make *shalom*. It's no wonder then that they typically escape persecution from the culture that they copy.

---

1. Willard, *Divine Conspiracy*, 300.
2. See 2 Tim 4:3–4.

The Fruit Tells All

> *By their fruit you will recognize them.* (Matt 7:16)

Broad-way preachers do bear a kind of fruit—the poisonous kind. It makes their hearers spiritually sick. They may identify as Christian and use biblical terminology, but their fruit is contaminated with falsehoods about the way heaven's kingdom comes to earth.

The earmark of a narrow way preacher is not a charismatic personality or how to look good in an expensive suit. The clearest sign is not a thunderous preaching tone, but an obedient life trajectory. Follow them only as they follow Christ, not how they toe their political party line or express rabid nationalistic pride. They might work miracles and punch out demons, but they don't know Jesus. Worse than that, Jesus doesn't know them (Matt 7:23)!

From a distance it's easy to mistake a wolf for a sheep or a bad tree for a good one. Sooner or later their true nature will present itself. The wolf will bare his teeth, and the poisonous tree will make people ill.

Broad-way preachers tend to claim their theology as the only right one or their political party the party of God. God always seems to be on their side against everyone on *the other side*. Preachers of the narrow way, on the other hand, demonstrate a meek and humble spirit, and can be trusted to point us in the direction of kingdom.

Will we turn the other cheek, love our enemies, refuse to bow to Mammon, and treat our neighbors like we want to be treated? If we want our "salt" to be salty and our "light" luminous, we must scrap these deceivers and choose to walk the narrow path alongside Jesus.

The Storm Will Tell

Therefore everyone who hears these words of mine and puts them into practice is like a wise man who built his house on the rock. The rain came down, the streams rose, and the winds blew and beat against that house; yet it did not fall, because it had its foundation on the rock. But everyone who hears these words of mine and does not put them into practice is like a foolish man who built his house on sand. The rain came down, the streams rose, and the winds blew and beat against that house, and it fell with a great crash.

—Matt 7:24–27

He began his Manifesto with eight startling "blesseds" and concludes it with the ominous warning: "and it fell with a great crash"! Everything in between his introductory and concluding remarks is his prescription on how to experience the blessedness and avoid the crash. Put his words into practice to enjoy and advance his kingdom or disregard his counsel and await calamity!

If it sounds serious, it's because it is.

I used to live in a typically foggy coastal town. There's a sign on one stretch of road, maybe fifty yards before you come to a stoplight that blinks in large letters: "Prepare to Stop!" When the fog is densest you can't see when the light turns red until it's too late to slow down to a stop. For years all the bulbs were burned out except the ones flashing: "Prepare . . . Prepare . . . Prepare . . ." It reminded me that God is always issuing a warning from heaven to be ready for a reckoning!

Preparing to stop before an intersection can save your life. Preparing for the storm may save your soul! The best and only way to ready yourself for it is to not just hear, and not just believe what Jesus says, but to *do it*.

Hearing and doing what he says guarantees an entirely different outcome than hearing and failing to act. Living *beatitudinally* gives us a much better chance of survival in the storm. It all boils down to *doing*.

In each of his three metaphors (two paths, two trees, and two houses) Jesus invites us to practice his kingdom way. Though from a distance the paths might have a similar appearance, they don't lead to the same place. The two varieties of fruit might taste the same, but they aren't equally nourishing. And when the storm arrives, one house will be washed away and the other will remain standing.

The preachers of the broad way convince their hearers to build anywhere they want and live any way they choose. *You don't really need a solid foundation, they say. Sand will do. It's not what you build upon that matters, but what it looks like once it's built. Appearance is paramount.*

But there's a storm coming that will impact every structure in its wake. One house will stand and the other will not. No matter how elegant it looks or how practical its floor plan, if it's not built squarely on the bedrock of obedience to God's kingship, when it's tested by the storm it will "fall with a great crash."

I know many people who used to follow Christ and now do not. I've also seen many churches and ministries that from the outside looked healthy and strong—until it was clear that they weren't. Somewhere along the way they crashed and burned. What happened? They stopped doing what Jesus told us to do. They had a house with rooms full of nice furniture and beautiful paintings on the walls, but they built on top of sand. They were more interested in their *appearance* than in their obedience. They looked fine for a while, but their self-determination caught up with them and they fell from grace.

The life you're building will be tested. There's no doubt about it. The "floods" will come from below, the "winds" will blow against all sides, and the "rain" will descend from above. It's what is *underneath* that matters most.

You're either standing on the rock or sinking in the sand. The issue at hand is not about following the right religion, but about ordering your life around the things Jesus prescribes. The storms will expose what is underneath. You might "believe" what he says but if you fail to act on it, then what you've built will fall. The storm will tell. But if your habit is to practice what he preaches, when the storms come, your house will survive.

He makes no guarantee that even a life submitted to his way will escape all suffering and injury in life's tempests. "The windows may get knocked out. A blue tarp may have to cover the shingle-less roof. Some sheetrock and carpet may have to be replaced, but the house remains firmly on its foundation."[1]

❦ ❦ ❦

The day I came to Christ I told my friend who led me to him, "I think God's gonna take me by the hand and show me how to do this." That was my best attempt to express how I was feeling at the moment. I wasn't trying to preemptively fend off any demands or dogma that she or anyone else would try to impose on me. Rather, my radical encounter with Jesus that day instilled in me a confidence that from then on, I would be inwardly determined.

There's always a choice whether or not to act on the Spirit's impulses within, and admittedly I've failed to follow up on those impulses more often than not. But I can truly say that when I've acted in concert with his commands, whatever storms have come my way (and I've faced a bunch of them over the years), with his moment-by-moment support, I've been able to weather each one.

❦ ❦ ❦

Lastly . . .

> When Jesus had finished saying these things, the crowds were amazed at his teaching, because he taught as one who had authority, and not as their teachers of the law. (Matt 7:28–29)

He finished the Sermon, and those who heard it sat there astonished. No surprise there. The Son of God gives humanity his best shot at describing how we were meant to live. Of course, they were amazed!

Jesus taught things that their teachers were unable or unwilling to teach. More than that, he possessed something they didn't. It wasn't

---

1. McBrayer, *Jesus Tribe*, 159.

bravado or sophistication. It wasn't training or skillful oratory. He had authority. Their teachers forfeited their moral authority by selling out to Rome for position and prosperity—something he never did. They preached either passive submission to their occupiers or violent overthrow, while he promoted humble, servant-like subversion.

If we find his words unpalatable, it's because we have such a damaged palate. He preached the kingdom of the narrow way, the *beatitudinal* way, which makes us uncomfortable, if not resistant. But we must resist our resistance and eschew our insistence on comfort. "The more you wrestle with the Beatitudes, the more they pull you into their depths. The deeper you dig, the more they yield."[2]

Yet his message is clearly *Made in Heaven* and conveys the ring of truth. His demands are "the very laws of our inmost being. When we discover them, we discover the natural way to live.... There is something within us that gives us the sense of this being the soul's homeland, that this is our native air, that we are made for this and for nothing else."[3]

Is this your reaction to Jesus' great Sermon on the Mount? If not, go back and read it again, and then again, until it feels like home, like you were made for it, like we were *all* made for it.

---

2. Eklund, *Beatitudes through the Ages*, 442.
3. Jones, *The Unshakable Kingdom and the Unchanging Person*, 219.

Acknowledgements

I HAVE MORE FRIENDS than I have any right to, many of which helped me in this publication in one way or another. Dan Wagner and Joseph McCroskey proofread every page, paragraph, word, and punctuation mark of my early drafts, and discovered an embarrassing number of typos and indecipherable sentences. Others read portions and offered constructive critique of my theological musings: Chris Matley, Michael Otvos, Scott and Andi Ann McCarrel, David Jensen, Nathanael Officer, Teri Peniston, Allison Thompson, Wayne Shaddock, David Paden, and Henry Bartlett. (Forgive my OG brain if I've overlooked anyone.)

As you can see from my bibliography, I'm a lover of the writings of others. Authors such as Tim Keller, E. Stanley Jones, Ron Sider, Walter Brueggemann, Shane Claiborne, David French, John Stott, D. Martin Lloyd-Jones, Clarence Jordan, Dallas Willard, and many others have made an inestimable contribution to my understanding of the kingdom of God and the Sermon on the Mount in particular.

I'd also like to thank my two beautiful granddaughters, Aria Joy and Esmé Davi. Right now they're only six years old, so they couldn't help with the writing directly. But spending time with these two delightful little humans playing hopscotch, reading fairy tales, and giggling a lot, keeps me from being up in my head all of my waking hours and helps point me back to the simplicity of childlikeness.

Lastly, giving a shoutout to Jesus may seem obligatory to some, nevertheless there's no sermon, not to mention, no "mount" without him! My meager understanding of his teaching pales by comparison to the purity of his very words birthed in heaven. Like an old tattered black and white photo of the Grand Canyon, my interpretations and applications of what he taught are paltry at best, if not flawed. I've loved him since the day he

Acknowledgements

found his way into my heart and I thank him for his Spirit's inspiration and assistance in writing this book.

As a pastor, I once stood up and announced that my message on that Sunday was going to be a reading of the best sermon ever preached. I paused to let the congregation guess what sermon that would be and who preached it. I could see the gears turning. Could it be Jonathan Edwards' "Sinners in the Hands of an Angry God" or one of Billy Graham's, John Wesley's, or Martin Luther King Jr's? And of course, I had them turn to Matthew's Gospel and began reading aloud chapters 5 through 7. When I finished, I gave a benedictory prayer and dismissed them without making any comments of my own. I figured how could anyone improve on Jesus?

This book was not an attempt to improve on his words, but a heartfelt effort to shed some light on them, with all the glory going to him.

Bibliography

Arnold, Eberhard. *The Prayer God Answers*. Walden, NY: Plough, 2016.
———. *Salt and Light: Living the Sermon on the Mount*. Walden, NY: Plough, 1998.
Ashford, Bruce Riley. *Every Square Inch: An Introduction to Cultural Engagement for Christians*. Bellingham, WA: Lexham, 2014.
Barclay, William. *The Beatitudes and the Lord's Prayer for Everyman*. New York: Harper & Row, 1975.
Bell, Rob, and Don Golden. *Jesus Wants to Save Christians: A Manifesto for the Church in Exile*. Grand Rapids: Zondervan, 2008.
Benne, Robert. *Good and Bad Ways to Think about Religion and Politics*. Grand Rapids: Eerdmans, 2010.
Bessenecker, Scott A. *How to Inherit the Earth*. Downers Grove, IL: InterVarsity, 2009.
———. *Overturning Tables: Freeing Missions from the Christian-Industrial Complex*. Downers Grove, IL: InterVarsity, 2014.
Bonhoeffer, Dietrich. *The Cost of Discipleship*. Macmillan, 1980.
———. *Letters and Papers from Prison*. New York: Touchstone, 1997.
Boyd, Greg. "Racism: Why Whites Have Trouble 'Getting It.'" https://christiansforsocialaction.org/resource/racism-why-whites-have-trouble-getting-it/.
Brooks, David. *The Second Mountain*. New York: Random House, 2019.
Brueggemann, Walter. *The Prophetic Imagination*. 40th ed. Minneapolis: Fortress, 2018.
Butler, Joshua Ryan, *The Skeletons in God's Closet*, Nashville, TN: Thomas Nelson, 2019.
Chambers, Oswald. *My Utmost for His Highest*. New York: Dodd, Mead, 1935.
Cho, Eugene. *Live Justly*. Portland, OR: Micah Challenge USA, 2014.
Claiborne, Shane. *Common Prayer: A Liturgy for Ordinary Radicals*. Grand Rapids: Zondervan, 2018.
Claiborne, Shane, and Chris Law. *Jesus For President: Politics for Ordinary Radicals*. Grand Rapids. Zondervan, 2008.
Dear, John. *The Beatitudes of Peace: Meditations on the Beatitudes, Peacemaking & the Spiritual Life*. New London, CT: Twenty-Third, 2016.
———. "Civil Disobedience and Discipleship to Jesus." *John Dear* (blog), 2019. http://johndear.org/civil-disobedience-and-discipleship-to-jesus/.
Eklund, Rebecca. *The Beatitudes through the Ages*. Grand Rapids: Eerdmans, 2021.
Engdahl, Derek. *The Great Chasm: How to Stop Our Wealth from Separating Us from the Poor and God*. Pomona, CA: Servant Partners, 2015.
Escobar, Kathy. *Down We Go: Living into the Wild Ways of Jesus*. Folsom, CA: Civitas, 2011.

Bibliography

Foster, Richard. *Celebration of Discipline: The Path to Spiritual Growth*. San Francisco: HarperCollins, 1998.

———. *Devotional Classics: Selected Readings for Individuals and Groups*. Rev. ed. New York: HarperOne, 2005.

———. *Freedom of Simplicity: Finding Harmony in a Complex World*. New York: HarperOne, 2005.

French, David. "Why Do They Hate Us?" *The Dispatch*, December 20, 2020. https://frenchpress.thedispatch.com/p/why-do-they-hate-us?r=1a7yf&fbclid=IwAR3s9FFK4xKUboy9oYlAIT5u3NawVgORBaCIEIYCG3YaiuGQG-B9ONx1-CQ.

Gates, Bill, and Melinda Gates. "Why We Swing for the Fences." *GatesNotes* (blog), February 10, 2020. https://www.gatesnotes.com/2020-Annual-Letter?utm_source=newsletter&utm_medium=email&utm_campaign=newsletter_axiosam&stream=top#ALChapter1.

Graham, Billy. "Does God Want Everyone to Be Rich?" https://billygraham.org/answer/does-god-really-want-everyone-to-be-rich/.

Greenfield, Craig. *Subversive Jesus: An Adventure in Justice, Mercy, and Faithfulness in a Broken World*. Grand Rapids: Zondervan, 2008.

———. "No, the Church Should Not Just Focus on 'Spiritual' Things." *Craig Greenfield* (blog), January 8, 2017. https://www.craiggreenfield.com/blog/over-spiritualized-gospel.

Hendricks, Obery. *The Politics of Jesus*. Manhattan, NY: Random House, 2006.

Heuertz, Christopher L., and Christine D. Pohl. *Friendship at the Margins: Discovering Mutuality in Service and Mission*. Downers Grove, IL: InterVarsity, 2010.

Howell, James C. *The Beatitudes for Today*. Louisville: Westminster John Knox, 2006.

Jones, E. Stanley. *A Song of Ascents: A Spiritual Autobiography*. Nashville, TN: Abington Press, 1968.

———. *The Unshakable Kingdom and the Unchanging Person*. Nashville, TN: Abigdon, 1972.

Jordan, Clarence. *Sermon on the Mount*. Valley Forge: Judson, 1980.

Keller, Timothy. *Generous Justice: How God's Grace Makes Us Just*. Toronto, Canada: Penguin Group, 2012.

———. *The Prodigal Prophet: Jonah and the Mystery of God's Mercy*. New York: Penguin, 2018.

King, Martin Luther, Jr. "A Knock at Midnight." https://kinginstitute.stanford.edu/king-papers/documents/knock-midnight.

———. "Letter from a Birmingham Jail." https://www.africa.upenn.edu/Articles_Gen/Letter_Birmingham.html.

———. "Loving Your Enemies." https://kinginstitute.stanford.edu/king-papers/documents/loving-your-enemies-sermon-delivered-dexter-avenue-baptist-church.

———. "Nonviolence and Racial Justice." https://kinginstitute.stanford.edu/king-papers/documents/nonviolence-and-racial-justice.

———. "Paul's Letter to American Christians." https://kinginstitute.stanford.edu/king-papers/documents/pauls-letter-american-christians-sermon-delivered-commission-ecumenical.

———. *The Strength to Love*. Gift edition. Minneapolis, MN: Fortress, 2010.

———. "When Peace Becomes Obnoxious." https://kinginstitute.stanford.edu/king-papers/documents/when-peace-becomes-obnoxious-sermon-delivered-18-march-1956-dexter-avenue.

Bibliography

Kraybill, Donald B. *The Upside-Down Kingdom.* Harrisonburg, VA: Herald, 2018.

Labberton, Mark. "Political Dealing: The Crisis of Evangelicalism." https://www.fuller.edu/posts/political-dealing-the-crisis-of-evangelicalism/.

———. *Still Evangelical? Insiders Reconsider Political, Social, and Theological Meaning.* Downers Grove, IL: InterVarsity, 2018.

Lamott, Anne. *Almost Everything.* New York: Random House, 2018.

Lee, Harper. *To Kill a Mockingbird.* New York: Harper Perennial, 2002.

Lloyd-Jones, D. M. *Studies in the Sermon on the Mount.* Grand Rapids: Eerdmans, 1971.

Mayfield, D. L. *The Myth of the American Dream: Reflections of Affluence, Autonomy, Safety, and Power.* Downers Grove, IL: InterVarsity, 2019.

McBrayer, Ronnie. *The Jesus Tribe: Following Christ in the Land of the Empire.* Macon, GA: Smyth & Helwys, 2011.

McNeel, Bekah. "Grieving Our Broken Border." *Christianity Today,* July 1, 2019. https://www.christianitytoday.com/ct/2019/july-web-only/grieving-our-broken-border-christian-leaders-lucado-lament.html.

Merton, Thomas. *New Seeds of Contemplation.* The Abbey of Gethsemani, 1961.

———. *The Nonviolent Alternative.* New York: Farrar, Straus & Giroux, 1971.

Moore, Charles, ed. *Following the Call: Living the Sermon on the Mount Together.* Walden, NY: Plough, 2021.

Peterson, Eugene. *Reversed Thunder.* New York: HarperOne, 1988.

———. *Run With the Horses.* Downers Grove, InterVarsity, 2019.

———. *Where Your Treasure Is: Psalms That Summon You from Self to Community.* Grand Rapids: Eerdmans, 1993.

"Pope Francis Urges Bishops to Defend Common Good in Madagascar." *Catholic News Agency,* September 27, 2019. https://www.catholicnewsagency.com/news/42207/pope-francis-urges-bishops-to-defend-common-good-in-madagascar.

Poplin, Mary. *Finding Calcutta: What Mother Teresa Taught Me About Work and Service.* Downers Grove, IL: InterVarsity, 2008.

Powell, John A. "Us vs Them: The Sinister Techniques of 'Othering'—and How to Avoid Them." *The Guardian,* November 8, 2017. https://www.theguardian.com/inequality/2017/nov/08/us-vs-them-the-sinister-techniques-of-othering-and-how-to-avoid-them.

Rohr, Richard. *Jesus' Plan for a New World: The Sermon on the Mount.* St. Anthony Messenger, 1996.

Romero, Oscar. *The Violence of Love.* Maryknoll, NY: Orbis, 2004.

Salvatierra, Alexia. *Faith-Rooted Organizing: Mobilizing the Church in Service to the World.* Downers Grove, IL: InterVarsity, 2014.

Scandrette, Mark. *Free: Spending Your Time And Money On What Matters Most.* Downers Grove, IL: InterVarsity, 2013.

———. *The Ninefold Path of Jesus: Hidden Wisdom of the Beatitudes.* Downers Grove, IL: InterVarsity, 2021.

Schiess, Kaitlyn. *The Liturgy of Politics: Spiritual Formation for the Sake of Our Neighbor.* Downers Grove, IL: InterVarsity, 2020.

Sider, Ronald J. *Speak Your Peace: What the Bible Says About Loving Our Enemies.* Harrisonburg, VA: Herald, 2020.

Stassen, Glen H. *Living the Sermon on the Mount: A Practical Hope for Grace and Deliverance.* San Francisco: Jossey-Bass, 2006.

BIBLIOGRAPHY

Stearns, Richard. *The Hole in Our Gospel: What Does God Expect of Us?* Nashville, TN: Thomas Nelson, 2009.

Stott, John. *The Message of the Sermon on the Mount.* Downers Grove, IL: InterVarsity, 1990.

Suttle, Tim. *An Evangelical Social Gospel?: Finding God's Story in the Midst of Extremes.* Eugene, OR: Cascade, 2011.

Temple, William. *Christianity & Social Order.* New York: Seabury, 1976.

Thoreau, Henry David. *Walden and Civil Disobedience.* Kolkata, India: Signet, 2012.

Thurman, Howard. *Deep Is the Hunger.* Richmond, IN: Friends United, 1973.

———. *Jesus and the Disinherited.* Nashvile, TN: Abingdon, 1976.

Tozer, A. W. *God's Pursuit of Man.* Chicago: Moody, 2015.

Volf, Miroslav. *Public Faith in Action: How to Engage with Commitment, Conviction, and Courage.* Grand Rapids: Brazos, 2016.

Wallis, Jim. *Christ in Crisis? Reclaiming Jesus in a Time of Fear, Hate, and Violence.* New York: HarperOne, 2019.

Washington, James Melvin, ed. *A Testament of Hope: The Essential Writings and Speeches of Martin Luther King, Jr.* San Francisco: HarperOne, 1991

Wehner, Peter. *The Death of Politics: How to Heal Our Frayed Republic After Trump.* New York: HarperOne, 2019.

Wiget, Barney. "'Man of Sorrows' Looking for Partners Acquainted with Grief." *Barney Wiget* (blog), May 27, 2016. https://barneywiget.com/2016/05/27/man-of-sorrows-looking-for-partners-acquainted-with-grief/.

———. "One-Scary-to-Pray-Prayer." *Barney Wiget* (blog), April 28, 2017. https://barneywiget.com/2017/04/28/one-scary-to-pray-prayer/.

———. "Recovering the Christian Art of the Lament." *Barney Wiget* (blog), May 30, 2017. https://barneywiget.com/2017/05/30/recovering-the-christian-art-of-the-lament/.

———. "Sometimes You Just Gotta Go Ahead and Cry!" *Barney Wiget* (blog), May 20, 2016. https://barneywiget.com/2016/05/20/sometimes-you-just-gotta-go-ahead-and-cry/.

Willard, Dallas. *The Divine Conspiracy: Rediscovering Our Hidden Life In God.* San Francisco: HarperCollins, 2014.

Wink, Walter. *Jesus and Nonviolence: A Third Way.* Minneapolis, MN: Augsburg Fortress, 2003.

Woodley, Randy. *Shalom and the Community of Creation: An Indigenous Vision.* Grand Rapids: Eerdmans, 2012.

Zahnd, Brian. *Postcards From Babylon: The Church in American Exile.* Columbia, SC: Spello, 2019.

www.ingramcontent.com/pod-product-compliance
Lightning Source LLC
Chambersburg PA
CBHW070737160426
43192CB00009B/1481